How to Develop Your Child's Gifts and Talents in Vocabulary

OTHER BOOKS BY MARTHA CHENEY:

How to Develop Your Child's Gifts and Talents in Reading
Monster Math, Book Two
Monster Math Puzzles & Games, 6–8
Gifted & Talented® Reading, Book Two, 4–6
Gifted & Talented® Math, Book Two, 4–6
Gifted & Talented® Puzzles & Games for Reading and Math, Book Two, 6–8
Gifted & Talented® Phonics, 4–6
Gifted & Talented® Phonics, 6–8
Gifted & Talented® Reading Comprehension, 6–8
Gifted & Talented® Math Puzzles & Games, 4–6
Gifted & Talented® Reading Puzzles & Games, 4–6

WITH DIANE BOCKWOLDT
Gifted & Talented® Puzzles & Games for Critical and Creative Thinking

WITH MARY HILL
Gifted & Talented® Atlas
Gifted & Talented® Almanac

WITH EVELYN PESIRI
Gifted & Talented® Dictionary
Gifted & Talented® Wordbook

WITH MARY CRON
Monster Math, Book One

HOW TO DEVELOP YOUR CHILD'S GIFTS AND TALENTS IN VOCABULARY

by

Martha Cheney

LOWELL HOUSE
LOS ANGELES

CONTEMPORARY BOOKS
CHICAGO

Library of Congress Cataloging-in-Publication Data

Cheney, Martha.
    How to develop your child's gifts and talents in vocabulary / by Martha Cheney.
        p.   cm.
    ISBN 1-56565-637-7
    1. Children—Language.   2. Language acquisition—Parent participation.   I. Title.
LB1139.L3C428 1997
372.44—dc21

                                            96-24052
                                                CIP

Copyright © 1997 by RGA Publishing Group. All rights reserved. No part of this work may be reproduced or transmitted in any form or by any means, electronic or mechanical, including photocopying or recording, or by any information storage or retrieval system, except as may be expressly permitted by the 1976 Copyright Act or in writing by the Publisher.

Requests for such permissions should be addressed to:
Lowell House
2020 Avenue of the Stars, Suite 300
Los Angeles, CA 90067

Lowell House books can be purchased at special discounts when ordered in bulk for premiums and special sales. Contact Department TC at the address above.

Publisher: Jack Artenstein
Associate Publisher, Lowell House Adult: Bud Sperry
Director of Publishing Services: Rena Copperman
Managing Editor: Maria Magallanes
Text design: Laurie Young
Illustrations © Dan Carsten

Manufactured in the United States of America
10 9 8 7 6 5 4 3 2 1

For Wesley and Daniel
my articulate & loquacious sons,
with love

CONTENTS

Introduction		ix
Chapter 1	How Children Acquire Language	3
Chapter 2	Learning New Words from Context	15
Chapter 3	Word Roots	35
Chapter 4	Prefixes and Suffixes	49
Chapter 5	Synonyms, Antonyms, and Homonyms	73
Chapter 6	Analogies	87
Chapter 7	Figures of Speech	97
Chapter 8	Where Do Words Come From?	107
Chapter 9	Games to Play with Words	121
Appendix	Words to Know	145

Introduction

THERE ARE HUNDREDS of thousands of words in a comprehensive English language dictionary! And this count does not include many of the specialized terms that relate to some particular field of study or endeavor. Doctors might use words like *ilioinguinal* and *thrombocytopenia* while in consultation with one another. Botanists or biologists might fling around terms such as *phylloxera* or *cephalochordate*. Lawyers might dictate, in stentorian tones, such gems as *interlocutory* or *exercitor*. Few people outside of a specific discipline need to devote time and energy to mastering this kind of lexicon, but everyone alive can benefit from having an improved vocabulary.

It is important to enhance your child's gifts and talents in the area of vocabulary in order to foster the child's success in personal relationships, success in school, and success in his or her chosen field. While a strong vocabulary alone will not guarantee the achievement of these goals that we all have for our children, it is one very important asset. In fact, studies show that an exceptionally strong vocabulary is a significant correlating characteristic of highly successful people, regardless of their fields, backgrounds, and educations.

How can this be so? We know that words are the building blocks of language. Language is the medium through which we think and communicate, making it a unique and invaluable treasure. A powerful vocabulary puts at our disposal a broad array of words from which to choose those that most accurately frame our ideas. These same words then allow us to precisely communicate the resulting thought to another person, either by speaking or writing. The more specific we can be in this process, the less chance there is for confusion and misunderstanding and the greater the opportunity for clarity and connection. The proper words make it possible to persuade and negotiate, to explain or elucidate. These are potent tools in both the personal and professional arenas.

A study of our language and the words that compose it will be helpful to parents who wish to accelerate and enhance a child's natural acquisition of new vocabulary. There are a variety of methods and techniques that will help to meet this goal, and these will be introduced and explained. These methods are most effective when used in combination.

First, of course, comes exposure to new words through the everyday use of language. This is the natural channel through which language is initially acquired. It is through this simple process that a firm foundation of language learning is constructed in the earliest years.

Reading becomes the next vehicle for bringing the child into contact with new words. Words that may not be in common usage in her daily sphere will be found in the books and stories that she reads or hears. Often the context in which the words appear will make their meanings clear, and with repeated exposure the child will come to own the words. Ultimately, this is probably the single most important means by which vocabulary is increased from school age on through adulthood.

However valuable it may be, this approach is limited in that it is not organized and therefore incomplete. It is helpful to look at words in a more orderly way, examining their roots and origins and grouping them by certain attributes. As students learn to analyze and categorize words they come to understand the relationships that exist between words. These relationships can help to give new words an immediate internal context, making them easier to learn and remember.

In addition to studying individual words, students need to be directly introduced to figures of speech and clichés. The words that make up these colorful phrases are shaded with meanings that go beyond the literal and are part of the magic of literature and culture. A close look at these devices will enable children to more fully interpret and appreciate what they read and hear.

HOW TO DEVELOP YOUR CHILD'S GIFTS AND TALENTS IN VOCABULARY

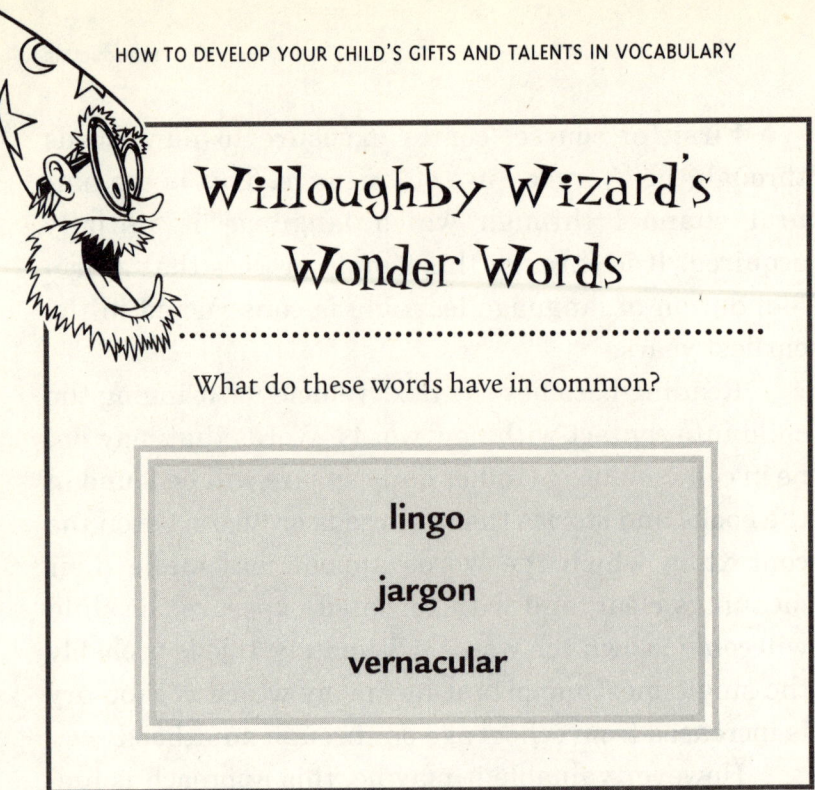

Willoughby Wizard's Wonder Words

What do these words have in common?

> lingo
>
> jargon
>
> vernacular

Finally, it can be enlightening to examine the origins of words and some of the changes that our language has experienced over the course of time. Some of our words have remained constant through centuries of cultural change, while others have become obsolete and have disappeared. At the same time, new words continually make their way into the language, keeping it alive and growing.

Use this book to help keep your child's vocabulary growing, too. Read it with your child, or just use the activities and exercises to entice him into the fascinating world of words. Be sure to share the Willoughby Wizard sidebars with your child and explore together the curiosities and challenges that Willoughby conjures up. Remember that an important objective is to foster a sense of enjoyment while exploring vocabulary. To this end, make sure to follow the interest level of your child. Don't ask her to do more than she wants to do in one sitting. Give her choices about which exercises and activities to complete. Use the word games in the final chapter liberally. They promote a wonderful sense of the intrinsic pleasures to be found in language, especially if you join in with enthusiasm.

HOW TO DEVELOP YOUR CHILD'S GIFTS AND TALENTS IN VOCABULARY

Chapter 1

How Children Acquire Language

A CHILD BEGINS the process of acquiring language in earliest infancy. At first, much of the communication between baby and parent is nonverbal. The warmth of cuddling, the soothing motions of rocking and walking, the familiar smell of his parents all assure him that he is safe. Slowly, the infant begins to recognize the smiling faces of family members and to smile in return. She cries when she is hungry or uncomfortable. So much is communicated before the baby has learned a single word!

These early months are extremely important ones in terms of language acquisition. Children need to be held, talked and sung to, smiled at, and played with in order to develop the motivation to learn language. As they grow they need to be exposed to many opportunities for exploration, so that they can gain understanding of the world around them.

Usually by about one year of age a child is beginning to use a few meaningful words on a regular basis. During the months that follow, it becomes apparent that he understands a great many more words than he uses, and can even respond to simple sentences that request or instruct him to do some particular action.

As she nears two years of age your child is taking on the task of learning grammar, and she begins to use words in combination. The more you talk with your child at this stage, the more opportunities she has to pick up the appropriate language patterns and to learn new words. Soon she will be using complete sentences and may have a speaking vocabulary of about nine hundred words and growing!

This incredible increase in vocabulary is a hallmark of the preschool years. You can make the most of this natural period of expansion by taking time to talk and read with your child every day. Remember, too, that a flood of questions will be released when the child has mastered the language tools necessary to frame them. This usually begins around the age of two and accelerates over the next several years. Be prepared to patiently encourage this natural curiosity by taking time to answer and discuss even the silliest and most repetitive questions. Spend as much time as you possibly can in conversation with your little one, regardless of her age.

By the age of five your child will likely be using as many as two thousand words, but remember that he has literally hundreds of thousands more to learn! Use

How Children Acquire Language

Willoughby Wizard's Wonder Words

What do the following words have in common?
Can you find more words to add to this list?

> **crimson**
>
> **azure**
>
> **mauve**
>
> **aquamarine**
>
> **vermilion**

books, pictures, and outings as jumping-off points for language and vocabulary development. Challenge yourself to stretch beyond the limits of the language you might use routinely to come up with words that are more specific or colorful to enhance each exploration you undertake with your child. For example, at the beach examine the sand and describe its qualities: gritty, fine, coarse, loose, and packed. The water can also be defined in a number of ways: as ocean, surf, waves, breakers, whitecaps, or tide. There are shells to identify by name and birds to watch as they soar through the air or squabble over scraps. When the sand is hot, it can sizzle, sear, and scorch. The cold water may be icy, chilly, or refreshing. Weave the words naturally into the conversation. Don't feel that you must talk down to your child, or limit your choice of words to simple ones that he or she already knows. Use rich language with your child and it will pay off. You may even find that you are having fun doing it!

Some other suggested activities and vocabulary that might flow from them follow. Of course, these are only suggestions, meant to help you get under way if you are feeling uncertain. They merely scratch the surface of the possibilities, so follow your own interests and those of your child. Your enjoyment is the key to success.

AROUND THE HOUSE
Cooking
Read a recipe together. Discuss the ingredients and talk about the utensils you will need to use. As you do each step be sure to talk about the process you are using: mix, stir, mince, whip, fold, cream, peel, chop, grate, beat, and so on.

Drawing and Painting
Experiment with dots and points, and lines that are thick, thin, straight, curved, wavy, and so on. Draw lots of shapes and discuss their names and what objects they resemble. What are the names of all the colors in the crayon box or paint tray? Make a list of all the different kinds of blue you can think of. Try using

How Children Acquire Language

Willoughby Wizard's Wonder Words

Onomatopoeia refers to words that are formed by imitating the sounds of actions or objects. Here are a few examples. Can you think of more?

clink	**coins in a pocket**
buzz	**a bumble bee**
tinkle	**ice cubes in a glass**
swish	**a horse's tail, or a windshield wiper**
hiss	**a snake**
mew	**a kitten**
crackle	**a bonfire, or dry leaves when you walk in them**
boom	**a cannon, or thunder**
sniffle	**what happens when you have a cold**

brushes and sponges to create drips, smears, dabs, and strokes. Be sure to describe each method as you use it.

Surround Sound

Ask your child to close his eyes and listen to the world for a minute or two. What does he hear? The rumble of a passing truck, the hum of a washing machine, the jangle of a telephone? Use descriptive names for each sound. Do similar exercises that utilize the senses of sight, taste, smell, and touch.

Backyard Explorers

Examine everything in your backyard with your child. What are the names of the plants and trees that are growing there? What kinds of animals can you find? Look in the grass for insects. Can you find a spider? How about birds? Discuss what each animal you see is doing. How does it move? How does it look?

Puppet Power

Purchase a few hand puppets or create your own out of felt, old socks, decorated paper bags, and so on. Help your child to dramatize favorite stories using the puppets. You can each choose a puppet and stage a conversation between the puppets. Sometimes slipping a puppet onto your hand has a surprising effect! You may find yourself using silly voices and some very creative vocabulary!

Collage Words

Look through magazines and newspapers to find words that describe your child and her interests. Cut out the

Willoughby Wizard's Wonder Words

On the left is a list of objects.
On the right is a list of people.
Match the objects to the people
who might use them.
As you go about your daily activities,
be aware of the people around you
and the tools and objects they use
in their work and play.

palette	**doctor**
whisk	**mechanic**
stethoscope	**teacher**
lariat	**artist**
text	**cowboy**
combine	**farmer**
wrench	**chef**

words and glue them onto a sheet of poster board. Cut out individual letters to spell her name, the names of her pets, and so on. Add magazine pictures, your own photos, or drawings to the collage.

OUT IN THE WORLD
The Park
The park is a wonderful place to explore words that relate to movement. You and your child can run, jump, twirl, crawl, roll, leap, and somersault across the grass. You can glide down the slide and sail through the air on a swing. Point out the actions of other people, such as a couple strolling by or a man dozing on the grass.

Museums
Museums are full of opportunities to meet new words. Exhibits ranging from dinosaurs to rocks and minerals to impressionist paintings are sure to introduce new ideas and thus new vocabulary to your child. Read the interpretive signs aloud as you look at each display. Discuss what you see and reinforce unfamiliar words by including them in your discussion. Look for books in the museum bookstore or your local library that relate to exhibits you visit. In this way you will extend the vocabulary encountered during the experience.

Tailor each visit to your child's age and interest level. Plan for frequent rest breaks and leave when your child shows signs of tiring. During the trip home ask your child to describe his or her favorite part of the day.

Willoughby Wizard's Wonder Words

There are special words for naming groups of particular animals. You might already know some of these words, but a few are bound to surprise you!

a gaggle of geese

a pride of lions

a pod of whales

a pack of wolves

a herd of cattle

a clutch of eggs

a covey of quail

a troop of monkeys

a swarm of bees

a sloth of bears

a muster of peacocks

HOW TO DEVELOP YOUR CHILD'S GIFTS AND TALENTS IN VOCABULARY

Willoughby Wizard's Wonder Words

Match the names of the animals on the left with the special names given to their young.

bear	gosling
fox	fawn
sheep	calf
chicken	lamb
horse	fledgling
bird	cub
goose	kit
cow	colt
deer	chick

The Mall

Even a shopping trip can be a source of vocabulary enrichment. Stop by window displays and talk about what you see. Are there mannequins in the display? What fabrics are used in the clothing you see? Are there opals and emeralds in a jewelry store window? Name and describe the objects you see, being as specific and colorful as possible. Encourage your child to do the same.

The Zoo

The zoo provides plenty of fun opportunities to learn about animals. Make sure to discuss the names of the animals and their countries of origin. Discuss the appearance and behavior of each animal. Are their skins woolly, leathery, armored, or scaly? Do they have hooves, paws, or claws? Are they energetic or drowsy?

Wherever you go and whatever you do with your child, **think vocabulary**. Talk with your child every day about the things you see and do together. As you become more aware of the words you use, your child's vocabulary will grow by leaps and bounds.

Chapter 2

Learning New Words from Context

PERHAPS THE MOST common and effective way of acquiring vocabulary is through extensive reading. As children read (or are read to) they are constantly meeting new words. Although you want to emphasize the reading of quality literature, remember that interesting vocabulary can be found in a variety of places. Comic books often use an extensive array of unusual words. Newspapers and magazines offer some excellent reading, but new words can also be encountered when reading the directions for assembling a model airplane or the back of a cereal box!

Often these words may be completely unfamiliar but will make sense to the reader or listener in the context of the written passage. It may take a number of exposures to the same word in a variety of contexts before the child has a full understanding of the word. Occasionally, it might be necessary to interrupt the reading to look up a word in the dictionary, but this is rare. Most of the time if the piece being read is within the comprehension range of the reader or listener, the surrounding text will sufficiently illuminate the word in question.

Sometimes the writer will use specific techniques that provide the reader with direct clues to the meaning of the word. One of these techniques is to actually define the word, as in the passage below:

> In colonial America a law breaker might be sentenced to several days in the pillory. A pillory was a wooden frame with openings through which the person to be punished would place his head and hands. The pillory was then locked, holding the person in place.

Another way to define a word for the reader is by example:

> There were several woodwinds in the band, including a flute and a clarinet.

The reader may not be familiar with the term *woodwinds,* but if she knows what a flute or a clarinet is, she will be able to extrapolate from this knowledge that *woodwinds* is an inclusive term for these and similar wind instruments.

Clues to the meaning of a word might be given by describing the word.

> The sweet, icy cold spumoni tasted wonderful to Francesca.

Though the reader may never have encountered the word *spumoni,* he will understand from this sentence that it means something cold and sweet to eat. This technique does not serve to directly define the word. There are many things that are cold and sweet, and the description does not reveal the fact that spumoni is an Italian ice-cream dessert. However, it does give the reader enough information to make sense of the passage, and perhaps will pique his curiosity sufficiently that he will seek the definition on his own.

Occasionally a writer will give some negative information about a word, using a clue that describes what the word is not, rather than explaining what it is.

> A spider is not an insect. It has eight legs instead of six and only two body parts.

This passage does not tell the reader that a spider is actually an arachnid, but it does let the reader know a spider differs from insects in some particular ways, thereby adding to her store of knowledge about both spiders and insects.

Another means of giving a negative clue is by incorporating a familiar antonym into the sentence that contrasts with the unknown word.

> The hardworking ant tried to warn the indolent grasshopper about the danger of his ways.

This sentence contrasts *hardworking,* which is a widely understood word, with the less familiar *indolent.* This contrast makes clear to the reader that *indolent* means the opposite of *hardworking.*

A final technique to examine is the use by a writer of a supporting word or phrase to define or describe a word. This phrase is called an appositive. It is usually set off by commas or parentheses and gives additional information about the word to which it relates.

> Thunderheads, large puffy storm clouds, began to appear over the mountains, and the hikers hurried back to camp.

From this sentence the reader can gather direct information about the meaning of the word *thunderheads* and glean some implications as well!

Use the exercises below to help your child practice identifying context clues. Be aware in your daily reading of the ways in which writers help readers to focus on word meanings. They are grouped into three categories. The first section involves examining pictures for context clues to give prereaders and beginning readers an opportunity to practice this important skill. The next section introduces some relatively simple vocabulary in context and challenges the reader to determine the meaning of each underlined word. The third section is identical to the second, except that it features a word list that is a bit more difficult.

Begin with the exercises you think are appropriate for your child. If they seem too difficult, drop back a level. If they seem too easy, go on to the next level. To extend this practice, encourage your child to articulate the meanings of new words he meets in his reading based on context clues.

EXERCISES FOR PREREADERS AND BEGINNING READERS

Young readers usually read stories that are supported by a good deal of illustration. Sometimes the clues contained in the pictures can be helpful in gaining understanding of the words and ideas presented in the story. In this section there are several pictures to examine for context clues. Discuss each picture with your child, using the questions provided as a guide.

A model discussion has been created to go with the first picture.

Buster Finds a Bone

Read the title and discuss the illustration on page 21 with your child. Ask your child the following questions:

Parent: What can you see in the picture?
Child: A dog, trees, apples, a bone.
Parent: What else?
Child: There's another dog hiding behind a tree. He looks mean.
Parent: Do you see a hole?
Child: Yes.
Parent: How about some dirt?
Child: Yes. And the happy dog has a collar, and there is a bird in the tree.
Parent: Who is Buster?
Child: The dog.
Parent: Which dog?
Child: The happy dog.
Parent: How do you know?

Child: Because he is digging up a bone. He found the bone.
Parent: Where is he?
Child: In a place with some trees.
Parent: A place where fruit trees are planted together is called an orchard. Buster is in an orchard.
Parent: What do you think might happen in this story?
Child: I think the mean dog is going to take the bone away from Buster.
Parent: You think he might try to steal the bone?
Child: Yes.

As you discuss the picture, try to bring up any vocabulary that might not be well known to your child, such as *orchard* and *steal*. When you are actually reading a picture book with your child, or asking her to read one to you, quickly skim it first to find words you think may be unfamiliar to your child. If possible, include the words in your picture discussion before beginning to read. This is a simple technique that is very helpful in smoothing the path to understanding new words. Try it using the pictures that follow. A few sample questions for you to ask your child are given with each picture to help launch your discussion.

A Surprise for Patty

What is happening in the picture?
Why are the children hiding?
Who is the party for?
How old is she?
What are some of the things the children might do at the party?

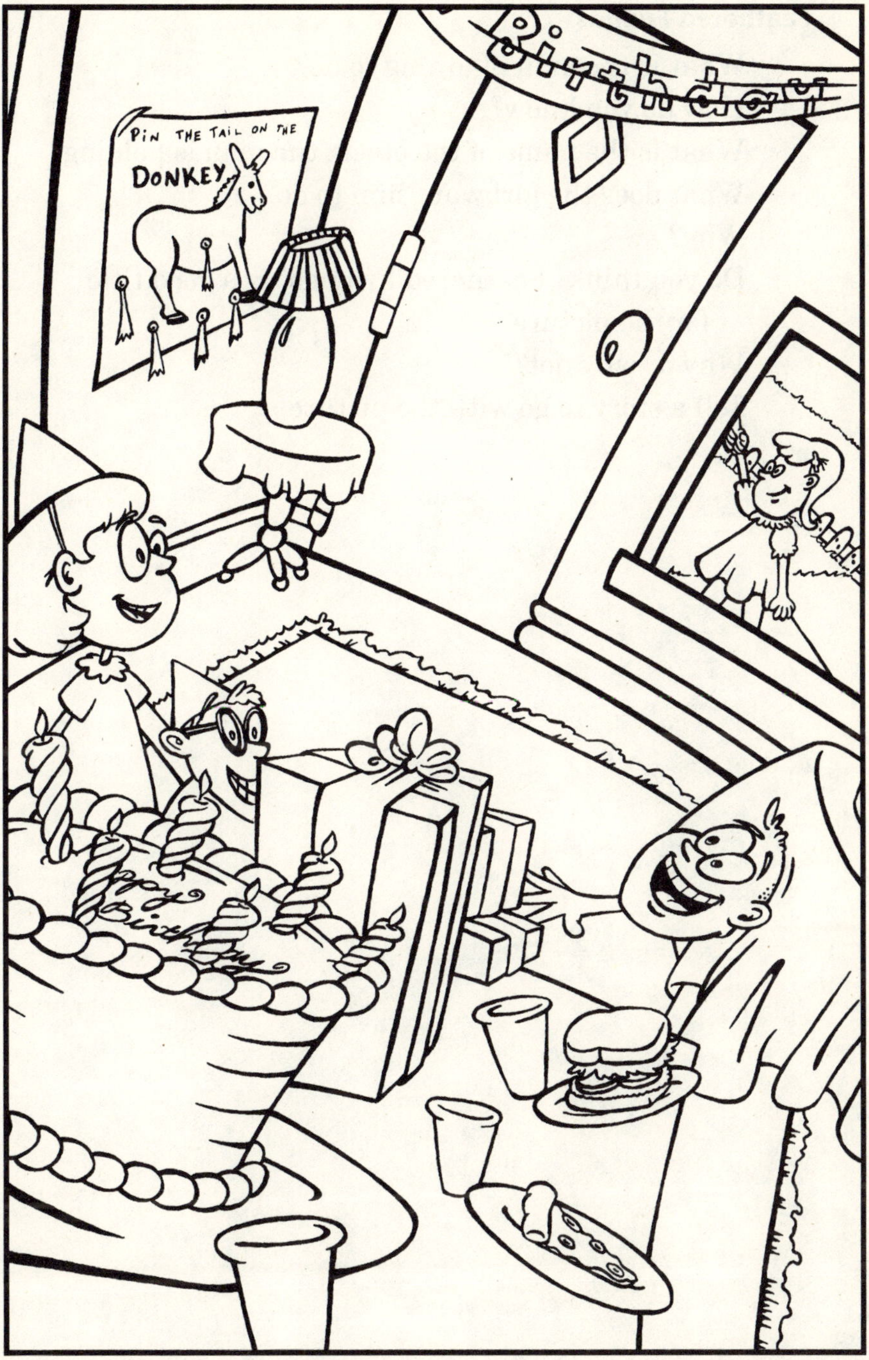
PIN THE TAIL ON THE
DONKEY
Birthday

Feathered Friends

What is the man planning to do?
How do you know?
What is the name of the object the man is holding?
What does the girl want him to do?
Why?
Do you think "Feathered Friends" is a good title for the picture?
Why or why not?
Tell a story to go with the picture.

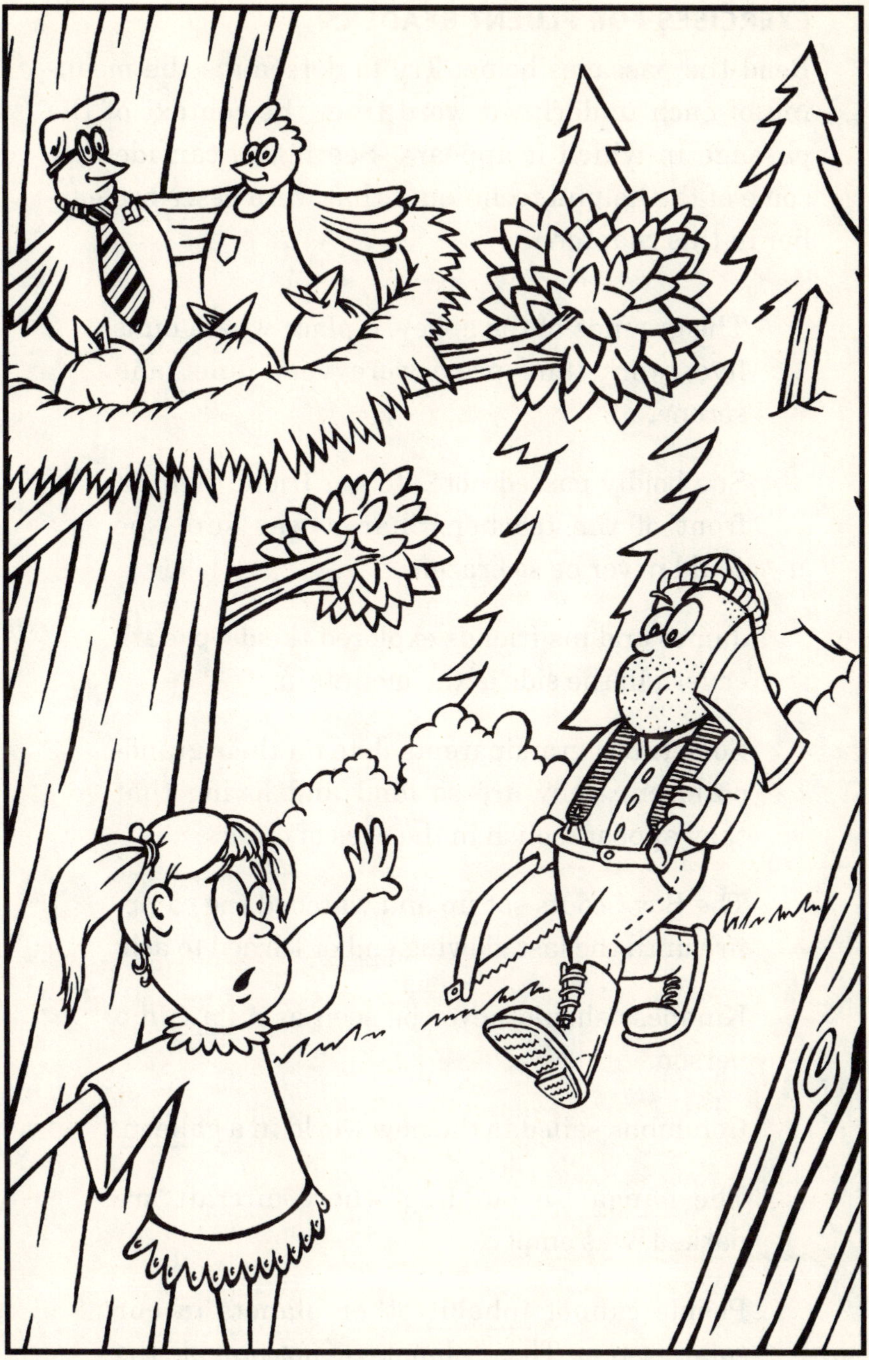

EXERCISES FOR FLUENT READERS

Read the passages below. Try to determine the meaning of each underlined word from the context of the passage in which it appears. See if you can identify some of the helpful techniques that were described earlier in this chapter.

The grounds of the abbey, a place where nuns live, work, and pray, were very quiet and serene.

Sue boldly passed notes to her friend right in front of the teacher. Sharon was sure she could never be so brazen.

James and his friends explored the deep, dark cavern in the side of the mountain.

Sometimes grandparents dote on their grandchildren. They are so fond and loving that they appear foolish in the eyes of others.

The Boy Scouts sat up and watched the campfire until the last glowing ember turned to ash.

Kindness should never be seen as a flaw in a person.

Columbus sailed to the new world in a galleon.

The hangar, a building where aircraft are parked, was empty.

People cannot inhabit other planets in our solar system. These planets do not provide the air, water, and temperature that humans must have in order to live.

Sarah's necklace was made of jade, a beautiful green stone.

"We have plenty of large logs," said Dad, "but we need a lot of kindling to get the fire started."

Carolyn put her dog into the tub for a bath. She rubbed soap all over him, creating a foamy lather.

The gardeners placed a heavy layer of mulch over the roots of the plants before the weather turned cold. Mulch is made of such materials as straw, leaves, or sawdust.

Susan was not nimble. She often tripped clumsily over her own feet.

Arthur thought the climb up Mount Jumbo was a terrible ordeal, but Delia enjoyed the hike.

As Mr. Smith got on the bus, he dropped several of his parcels. The other passengers helped him pick up the packages.

In her quest for a championship the young diver had to practice for many hours.

The cowboy held the reins, the leather straps used to guide a horse, loosely in his left hand.

The mother cat picked up her kitten by the scruff of his neck and carried him to the barn. The scruff is the loose skin on the back of the neck.

The tightrope walker made sure the rope was taut instead of loose before he set out across it.

A degree is the unit of measure used to describe temperature.

The steam from the kettle formed a vapor, which filled the kitchen.

Glenn was filled with wrath, a deep and terrible anger, when he saw the robber push the old lady to the ground and take her purse.

Charlie and Beth are having fun at summer camp, but they miss their families and yearn for letters from home.

Jennifer is known as the zany member of the group. She is always clowning around.

**EXERCISES FOR
MORE ADVANCED READERS**

The king decided to abdicate his throne. He was tired of being in charge.

The speaker was not known for his brevity. His speeches seemed to last forever.

Martin found a secret hiding place for his treasures. He was sure no one could locate his cache.

The diligent student was more successful than the lazy one.

Next month our magazine subscription will expire, or come to an end.

The basketball player committed a flagrant foul. He pushed another player right in front of an official.

The dragonfly's gossamer wings seemed too light and filmy to support its weight.

It was necessary to use a crane to hoist, or lift, the heavy cargo onto the ship.

Maria made several mistakes when she added the column of numbers, but her calculator was infallible.

The winning team was jubilant, while the losers were sad and downcast.

Grandmother polished the silver teapot to a deep luster. It had never been so shiny, even when new.

Babies like to mimic the expressions they see on the faces of people around them. They also try to copy the sounds and words that they hear.

Many birds are active during the day, but some, like owls, are nocturnal.

Jamie did not consider herself to be obtuse, but she had to struggle to understand algebra.

The stew smelled strongly of garlic. The odor was pungent but pleasant.

Kelly was in a quandary. She couldn't decide which dress to buy for the dance.

My older brother would sometimes ridicule me in front of my friends. When he made fun of me, I would laugh, even though I felt more like crying.

There was nothing sinister about Mrs. Mortimer, even though she always dressed in black and looked rather frightening.

This tributary, or small river, empties into the Columbia River.

The pots, pans, spoons, and other utensils need to be washed and put away.

Elizabeth was quiet and shy, but Brenda was lively and vivacious.

"Oh, you poor, lonely little waif," Colin whispered to the stray puppy he found on his front porch.

We celebrate the yuletide with our own special traditions. The yuletide is the Christmas season.

At the zenith of his career Mr. Patterson was the most famous director in Hollywood.

EXERCISES FOR ALL READING LEVELS

Ask your child to supply a word or a phrase for each blank space in the passages below. There are many possible answers. Encourage the older child to come up with multiple responses for each blank. Suggest that he try to find words that are as descriptive or creative as possible. You can also find a noun in the dictionary to fill in the first blank and then challenge your child to fill in the remaining blanks in a way that relates to that noun.

For example, if the word *boomerang* is the noun selected, the blanks might be completed as follows:

Julie found a *boomerang* in the *closet*. It was *brown* and *wooden*. She decided to *throw* it.

Julie found a _____ in the _____. It was _____ and _____. She decided to _____ it.

When Kenny went to the _____, he saw a _____ and a _____. He heard _____. He smelled the _____.

Wally climbed onto the _____. It began to _____. Wally felt _____ and _____.

HOW TO DEVELOP YOUR CHILD'S GIFTS AND TALENTS IN VOCABULARY

Willoughby Wizard's Wonder Words

Use context to find the picture that illustrates each underlined word.

Jacob put a <u>bulb</u> in the light fixture.

Shelley's uncle made her a beautiful spinning <u>top</u> to play with.

32

Learning New Words from Context

Mr. Phillips bought three bars of soap for $1.00.

Chapter 3

Word Roots

SCHOLARS WHO HAVE studied the evolution of language believe that the earliest identifiable ancestor of our language was an unwritten language called Indo-European. It was given this name because it appears to be the forerunner of the languages spoken in modern-day India and Europe. The people who spoke this language were nomads who roamed across Europe for thousands of years, taking their language with them as they traveled.

Eventually, one tribe of these Indo-European people came to settle in Britain. They were called Celts, and with their arrival the evolution of the English language began. The Celts fought the more primitive people they found living in the British Isles and gained dominance for many years.

When the Romans conquered Britain about two thousand years ago, overpowering the Celts, they brought with them their own language—Latin. The Romans maintained their control over Britain for four hundred years. When the Romans withdrew, a number of Germanic tribes, including the Angles, Saxons, and Jutes, rushed in to fill the void. These tribes conquered Britain, and the most successful of the tribes, the Angles, eventually gave England its name and its language—English. The English spoken by the Angles and Saxons is not the same language we speak today. It is referred to as Old English.

In the year 1066 the Normans invaded England and defeated the Anglo-Saxons. They brought with them the French language, which had developed from the Latin of the Romans. French became the official language of the land, spoken by the conquerors who took over the positions of wealth and influence. However, the common people held fast to their language and kept it in use. Over a period of several hundred years the Normans intermingled with the Anglo-Saxons, and English reemerged as the predominant language of the land. Of course, by this time the language had changed a great deal. The influence of the Normans was seen in the many words with Latin roots that had crept into the language. Also, during this period Latin was the language of the church and of scholars around the world, further strengthening the influence of this language on the development of English. The language that emerged from this period is known as Middle English.

Middle English would be difficult for a present-day

American to read and understand, although many of the words would be recognizable. It took about three hundred years for the language to evolve from Middle English into the Modern English that has now been in use for several centuries. And although word meanings continue to change and new words are added to the language at a rapid pace, we can read the works of Shakespeare in their original form and understand them easily, demonstrating that Modern English is a mature and durable language.

In our study of vocabulary it is fun as well as useful to examine the roots of the words that make up Modern English. When the student knows the meanings of many of the root portions of words, she can then apply this knowledge to new words that she meets. When she sees a long and unfamiliar word, she will not be daunted! She can use her knowledge of word roots to analyze each portion of the word and generally come up with a pretty good idea of what the parts of the word combine to mean. For example, if she encounters the word *bibliomania,* she will recognize *biblio* as "book" and *mania* as "madness" and realize that the word means "a madness for books."

You should also be aware that a good dictionary will provide information about the etymology of words. After each word entry, look for abbreviations such as *L.* for Latin or *Fr.* for French, followed by the word in that language from which the word entry derives. The symbol <, meaning "comes from," may be used to indicate derivations.

Explore some word roots with your child by completing the following exercises together. Devote just a few minutes a day to the exercises. Remember that your goal is to familiarize your child with these roots, not to force him to memorize them. Use the list of word roots at the end of this chapter as a reference, looking up the meanings of roots you run across in your daily reading.

**EXERICISES FOR EXPLORING
THE MEANINGS OF WORD ROOTS**

Find the one word that will make sense in each blank. This word will give you the meaning of the root. Try to make up some more sentences of your own, leaving a blank for the root.

astro
An astronaut is someone who travels among the _____.
Astrology is the telling of fortunes using the _____ for guidance.

aud
An audience comes to see and _____ a performance.
In a good auditorium, it is easy to _____ the speaker.

cycl
Each wheel on a bicycle is shaped like a _____.
A cyclone is formed when high winds whirl in a _____.

div
To divide the money, the brothers placed it in two _____ piles.
When people divorce, they _____ from each other.

graph
When a famous actor signs an autograph, he _____ his name.
When an author _____ a book about someone's life, it is called a biography.

loc
The location of an object is the _____ where it can be found.
Local news is the news that relates to a particular _____ and the people who live there.

man
A manual is sometimes called a _____ book.
A manicure includes the trimming and polishing of the nails on the _____.

marin
A submarine is a boat that travels deep in the ocean or _____.
A marina is a docking area for boats that is in or near the _____.

meter
A thermometer can _____ temperature.
Diameter is used to _____ the distance across a circle or a sphere.

min
A miniature poodle is very _____.
A minor actor in a production has a _____ role.

multi
A multicolored coat has _____ different colors.
It takes a great _____ people to form a multitude.

phon
Phonics is the study of the _____ of letters.
When you talk on the telephone, the _____ of your voice is transmitted to the other person.

port
Something that is portable is easy to _____.
Vehicles are used to _____ people and things from place to place.

spect
A spectator _____ at the event he has come to see.

An inspector _____ carefully at the objects produced at the factory to make sure they are well made.

therm

A thermostat is used to regulate _____.
If you put soup in a thermos bottle, the _____ will not escape.

Dig for Roots!

Choose one word root and use a dictionary to find as many words containing that root as you can. Post a list of the words you find. Be on the lookout for words based on that root while you are reading. Add these to your list. When you feel you have exhausted one root, begin a search for another. Encourage your child to illustrate the list.

Create-a-Word

Make up new words using roots that have become familiar to your child. Announce the root you are using and make up a definition for each of your created words. Challenge your child to come up with each word you have in mind. For example, a small brown paper bag might be a "lunchport"; a report card might become a "gradeometer."

Word Tree

Help your child make a poster showing the simple outline of a tree. Draw the roots, trunk, and bare branches. On the root portion write a common word root. On the trunk write the meaning of the root. Cut out leaf shapes from construction paper. Write a word that incorporates the root on each leaf. Glue the leaves to the tree. Whenever you think of another word with that root, add it to your tree. Encourage your child to find additional words, too.

REFERENCE LIST OF WORD ROOTS

This list of word roots is extensive but by no means comprehensive. Use it as a reference to help you and your child understand the meanings of words and parts of words. Use it as a springboard for conversation or wordplay. Think of as many words using each root as you can. Use a dictionary if you like. Make up sentences or stories with your child using the words you find.

Root	Meaning	Examples
acro	highest	acrobat, acrophobia
act	move, do	actor, activate
aer	air	aeroplane, aerial
agr	field	agriculture, agrarian
alpha	first, beginning	alpha, alphabet
alt	high	altitude, exalted
am, amor	love	amiable, amorous
ambul, ambl	walk	ambulance, amble
anim	mind or spirit	animal, animation
anni, annu	year	anniversary, annual
anthrop	man	anthropology, anthropoid

Word Roots

Root	Meaning	Examples
aqua, aque	water	aquarium, aqueduct
arbitr	consider, judge	arbitration, arbitrary
arbor	tree	arbor, arboreal
arch	rule, chief	architect, monarch
arm	weapon	armor, arms
astro, aster	star	astronaut, asterisk
athl	contest	athlete, decathlon
aud	hear	audible, auditorium
auto	self	autobiography, autograph
avi	bird	aviator, aviary
belli	war	rebellion, belligerent
bene	good, well	benefit, benefactor
bibl	book	Bible, bibliography
bio	life	biography, biology
brev	brief	abbreviate, brevity
cal	hot	calorie, caldron
cand	glow	candle, incandescent
cap	head	captain, capital
cav	hollow	cave, cavern
cen	burn	incense, incendiary
cens	judge	censor, census
cent	hundred	cent, century
centr	center	central, centrifugal
cept	receive, take	accept, reception
cert	make clear	certain, certificate
chron	time	chronic, chronology
cide	kill	pesticide, suicide
circ	ring	circle, circus
civ	citizen	civilian, civilization
clar	clear	clarify, declare

Root	Meaning	Examples
color	conceal, cover	colorful, Colorado
corp	body	corpse, incorporate
cracy	government	democracy, bureaucracy
cred	belief	credo, credible
crim	judge, accuse	criminal, incriminating
cult	cultivate, worship	agriculture, cult
cum	pile up	accumulate, cumulus
cur	care	manicure, cure
cycl	circle, wheel	cycle, cyclone
dem	people	democracy, epidemic
dent	tooth	dental, dentist
derm	skin	dermatology, epidermis
dic, dict	say	predict, verdict
div	separate	divide, divorce
don	give	donation, pardon
duc, duct	lead	education, conduct
dur	hard	endure, durable
equ	equal	equality, equation
fac	make	factory, facsimile
fer	carry	transfer, ferry
fin	end	final, finish
fix	fasten	fixture, prefix
flam	flame	inflame, flammable
flor	flower	florist, flora
flu	flow	fluent, fluid
fol	leaf	foliage, portfolio
form	shape	reform, transform
fort	strong	fort, fortify

Root	Meaning	Examples
frag, fract	broken	fragment, fraction
geo	earth	geography, geological
gon	angle	polygon, pentagon
grad	step	graduate, gradual
gram	letter	monogram, telegram
graph	write, record	autograph, pictograph
grat	thanks	gratitude, congratulations
greg	gather, flock	congregate, aggregate
heir, her	receive	heirloom, inherit
homo	same	homonym, homogenized
hos	host	hospital, hostess
hydr	water	hydrant, dehydrated
ign	fire	ignite, igneous
ject	throw	project, reject
jour	daily, day	journal, journey
ju	law	judge, judicious
juven	young	juvenile, rejuvenate
lat	side	lateral, bilateral
leg	law	legal, legislature
leg	read	legible, legend
liber	free	liberate, liberal
liqu	liquid	liquor, liquefy
loc	place	location, locale
luc	light	lucid, translucent
lum	light	illuminate, luminous
man	hand	manicure, manual
mand	order	demand, command
mania	madness	maniac, pyromania
mari	sea	marine, maritime

Root	Meaning	Examples
med	middle	medium, mediocre
merc	trade	mercantile, merchandise
meter	measure	meter, altimeter
mid	center	middle, midterm
migr	move	migrant, migrate
milit	soldier	military, militia
min	small	minute, minimum
miss	send	mission, missive
mit	send	commit, transmit
mob	move	mobile, automobile
mort	death	mortuary, mortal
mot	move	motor, promote
mov	move	movie, movable
nat	born	native, innate
nav	ship	navy, navigate
nov	new	novelty, novice
numer	count	numerous, numeral
onym	name	synonym, pseudonym
ortho	straight	orthodontist, orthodox
ova	egg	oval, ovary
par	equal	compare, parity
ped	foot	pedal, pedestrian
pel	push	repel, propel
pend	hang	pendulum, appendix
phon	sound	phonics, telephone
port	carry	transport, portable
popul	people	population, popular
prim	first	primary, primitive
pup	child	puppy, pupil

Word Roots

Root	Meaning	Examples
ras, raz	scrape	erase, razor
sacr	holy	sacrifice, sacred
scop	watch	microscopic, telescope
scri	write	script, inscribe
sect	cut	insect, dissect
sen	old	senior, senile
serv	save	conservation, preserve
simil, simul	same	similar, simultaneous
sol	alone	solitary, solo
solv	loosen	resolve, dissolve
spect	look	inspect, spectacle
stru	build	construction, structure
tele	distant	telephone, television
temp	time	temporary, contemporary
terra	earth	terrace, territory
therm	heat	thermal, thermometer
tract	pull	tractor, extract
urb	city	urban, suburb
vaca	empty	vacation, vacant
val	strong	value, valid
vari	different	varied, variety
veh	carry	vehicle, conveyor
ver	truth	veracity, verdict
verb	word	verbal, proverb
vid, vis	see	video, visual

HOW TO DEVELOP YOUR CHILD'S GIFTS AND TALENTS IN VOCABULARY

Root	Meaning	Examples
vict	conquer	victor, convict
vit	life	vital, vitamin
viv	live	survive, vivacious
voc	voice	vocal, invocation
volv	roll	revolve, revolution
zo	animal	zoo, protozoa

Chapter 4

Prefixes and Suffixes

PREFIXES AND SUFFIXES, along with word roots, are the components from which many words are built. The child who has some understanding of the meanings of these components can put them together to form new words or take them apart to examine longer, unknown words in a systematic manner.

Prefixes are word components that are added to the beginning of a root word to clarify or add something to the meaning of the word. Your child can refer to the prefix list at the end of this chapter when she has a question about the meaning of a particular prefix that she encounters in her reading.

EXERCISES FOR PRACTICE WITH PREFIXES

Find the one word that will make sense in each blank. This word will give you the meaning of the prefix. Try to make up some more sentences of your own, leaving a blank for the word that gives the meaning of each prefix.

anti
We take an antibiotic to fight _____ harmful germs.
We put antifreeze in our cars to protect _____ freezing.

be
To belittle someone is to _____ them feel small.
To becalm someone is to _____ them be still and quiet.

contra
When we contradict someone, we speak _____ something they have said.
Someone who is contrary seems to be _____ everything!

dis
A dog who is disobedient does _____ obey.
A dishonest person does _____ tell the truth.

Prefixes and Suffixes

ex

Exit is another word for the way _____ of a room or a building.

When you exhale, you are breathing air _____ of your lungs.

extra

An extraterrestrial comes from _____ the planet earth.

An extraordinary event is _____ the usual or ordinary.

il

If your writing is illegible, then I will _____ be able to read it.

An illegal act is one that is _____ permitted by law.

in

When you inhale, you take air _____ your lungs.

When you include someone in your conversation, you draw them _____ it.

inter

The intermission came _____ the first and second acts of the play.

The intercom allows for communication _____ the office and the classroom.

micro

A microscope makes it possible to see things that are very _____.

A microbe is an organism that is very _____.

mid
Midnight is the _____ of the night.
A boat that is midstream is in the _____ of the water.

pre
When you make a prediction, you are saying what you think will happen _____ an event actually takes place.
Premeditation means to think about something _____ you do it.

re
When a store gives you a refund, you get your money _____.
If you repay a debt, you give the money _____ to the person who lent it to you.

sub
A submarine travels _____ the water.
A subway is a train that travels _____ the ground.

trans
The transcontinental railroad went all the way _____ the continent.
A transmitter sends signals _____ a great distance.

As you may have noticed there are many prefixes that have the same or similar meanings. There are quite a few prefixes that serve to form negative words. Some of the most common are *a, dis, im, in, ir, non,* and *un*. In the exercises that follow, fill in each blank with a word made negative by the addition of one of these prefixes. The word should mean the same thing as the underlined phrase in each exercise. Note that the prefixes, though they have similar meanings, are not usually interchangeable. We speak of someone who is unhappy, but not dishappy. An action might be improper, but never inproper. Use a dictionary to check your answers.

> The girls were <u>not kind</u> to each other. They were _____.
>
> The volcano was <u>not active</u>. It was _____.
>
> Judy bought a bracelet that was <u>not expensive</u>. It was _____.
>
> Mara was <u>not definite</u> about her plans. Her plans were _____.
>
> Joe knew it was <u>not possible</u> for him to lift the heavy weight. It was _____.
>
> Martin's sculpture was <u>not symmetrical</u>. His teacher said that it was _____.
>
> The judge said that the accused man could not stand trial because he was <u>not sane</u>. The court declared him to be _____.

Sarah cut two slices of cake that were <u>not equal</u> in size. The slices were _____.

Mrs. Lambert said that measurements that were <u>not exact</u> would ruin the recipe. She did not like _____ measurements.

The children were crowded into a hot, stuffy auditorium. They were <u>not comfortable</u>. They were _____.

The conduct of the class was <u>not orderly</u>. It was _____.

After Joan hit her head, she was <u>not conscious</u>. She was _____.

The Price family was <u>not pleased</u> with the new car. They were _____.

Several students did not return their library books. The librarian felt that their behavior was <u>not responsible</u>. The students' behavior was _____.

The books were <u>not fiction</u>. They were _____.

The tests showed that Mr. Jensen's heartbeat was <u>not regular</u>. It was _____.

At the party, Rebecca insisted on being served first even though she knew it was <u>not polite</u>. Rebecca's behavior was _____.

REFERENCE LIST OF PREFIXES

The following is a list of some of the most commonly used prefixes. There are many, many others. As you and your child think of or discover additional prefixes, add them to the list.

Prefix	Meaning	Examples
a	on	aboard, atop
a	not, without	atheist, amoral
ab	off, away	abduct, abnormal
ad	toward, near	adverb, adhere
ambi	both, around	ambidextrous, ambiguous
ante	before	antebellum, antechamber
anti	against	antifreeze, antibiotic
auto	self	autograph, autobiography
be	make	becalm, belittle
bene	good	benefit, benevolent
com	together	combine, companionship
con	with	connect, confer
contra, contro	against	contrary, contradict, controversy
counter	opposite	counterbalance, counterclockwise
de	down, opposite	descend, dehydrate
dis	not	disloyal, disobedient
dis	opposite, apart	disappear, disarm
e	out	evict, edict
en	in	enrage, enroll

HOW TO DEVELOP YOUR CHILD'S GIFTS AND TALENTS IN VOCABULARY

Prefix	Meaning	Examples
ex	out	exit, extol
extra	outside	extraordinary, extraterrestrial
for	prohibit, omit	forbid, forget
fore	beforehand	forearm, forebode
hyper	over	hypertension, hyperbole
hypo	under, too little	hypodermic, hypotension
il	not	illiterate, illegible
im	into	immigrant, import
im	not	imperfect, impossible
in	not	inexact, infinite
in	into	infuse, install
inter	between	international, intermission
intra, intro	within	intramural, introvert, introduction
ir	not	irresponsible, irregular
mal	bad	malignant, malodorous
mega	large	megaphone, megaton
micro	small	microscope, microphone
mid	middle	midway, midsummer
mis	wrong, bad	misdemeanor, mishap
multi	many	multiple, multimillion
neo	new	neoclassic, neophyte
non	not	nonsense, nonskid
off	away from	offhand, offshore
omni	all	omnivorous, omnipotent

Prefixes and Suffixes

Prefix	Meaning	Examples
on	on	onlooker, oncoming
out	beyond	outshine, outdo
out	outside	outdoors, outlaw
over	too much, extra	overrun, overpay
poly	many	polygon, polyglot
post	after	postpone, postscript
pre	before	preheat, prehistoric
pro	in favor of	proponent, proslavery
pro	forward, front	prospect, program
pseudo	false	pseudonym, pseudopod
re	again	rebirth, recall
re	back	refund, recoil
semi	half, partly	semicircle, semicolon
sub	under, below	submarine, subconscious
super	over, beyond	supernatural, supercharge
trans	across, over	transcontinental, transport
un	not	untroubled, unhappy
under	below	underwater, underwrite
up	up, upward	uphold, upkeep
with	back, against	withdraw, withhold

ADDITIONAL PREFIXES

_____ _____ _____
_____ _____ _____
_____ _____ _____
_____ _____ _____
_____ _____ _____

A special group of prefixes refers to number. The most common of these are listed below, along with some examples of words that include them.

One

mono-	*uni-*
monarch	unicycle
monochrome	unicorn
monocle	unify
monogram	uniped
monogamy	union
monopoly	unit
monotone	unite
monotheist	universe
monologue	unilateral

Two

bi-	*di-*	*du-, dua-, duo-*
biceps	diagonal	dual
bicuspid	dialogue	duel
bicycle	dichotomy	duet
bifocal	dichromatic	duo
biped	dilemma	duplex
biplane	dimorphous	
bisect	diode	
biweekly		

Prefixes and Suffixes

Three

tri-
triangle
triceps
tricolor
tricuspid
tricycle
trident
trimester
trinity
triple
triplet
tripod
triptych
triumverate
trivet

Four

quad-, quart-, quat-
quadrangle
quadrant
quadruped
quadruple
quart
quarter
quarterly
quartet
quatrefoil

Five

quint-
quintet
quintuple
quintuplet

pent-
pentagon
pentatonic

Six

sex-
sextet
sextuple
sextuplet

hex-
hexagon
hexapod

59

Seven

sept-
September
septet
septuple
septuplet

Eight

oct-, octa-, octo-
octagon
octave
octet
October
octopus
octuple

Nine

nona-, novem-
nonagenarian
nonagon
November

Ten

dec-, deca-
decade
decagon
decathlon
December
decibel
decimal

One Hundred

cent-, centi-
cent
centennial
centimeter
centipede
century

EXERCISES FOR PRACTICE WITH SUFFIXES

Suffixes are word components that are added to the end of a root word and generally serve to change the part of speech of the word. For example, we use a suffix *-or* to change the verb *sail* to the noun *sailor.* We add a suffix *-ly* to change the adjective *sweet* into the adverb *sweetly.*

Explore the exercises below with your child. After each section, ask him to describe to you the change that takes place when a particular suffix is added to a word.

By examining some familiar words, he should be able to infer the meanings of these word endings.

What do the suffixes *er* and *or* mean?

    painter   A painter is a _____ paints.
    farmer   A farmer is a _____ farms.
    actor   An actor is a _____ acts.
    dancer   A dancer is a _____ dances.
    baker   A baker is a _____ bakes.
    runner   A runner is a _____ runs.
    swimmer A swimmer is a _____ swims.
    teacher   A teacher is a _____ teaches.

Sometimes the suffix **er** has another meaning. Can you figure out what it is?

    The night got darker. That means it got _____ dark.

    Marie was happier at school after she made a friend. She was _____ happy.

    The twins grew sleepier as the hours past. They grew _____ sleepy.

    The children swam in deeper water. The water they swam in was _____ deep.

    Susan thought her dress was prettier than Simone's. Susan thought her dress was _____ pretty.

Mr. Forbes put flowers on the table to make it fancier. He made the table _____ fancy.

Sharon copied her work over so that it would be neater. She wanted it to be _____ neat.

The test was tougher than Celeste expected it to be. The test was _____ tough.

Brandon thought the test was easy. He feels he is smarter than Celeste. He thinks he is _____ smart.

What does the suffix *less* mean?

fearless	A woman who is fearless is _____ fear.
hopeless	A situation that is hopeless is _____ hope.
friendless	A boy who is friendless is _____ friends.
bottomless	A pit that is bottomless is _____ a bottom.
toothless	A dog that is toothless is _____ teeth.
endless	A view that is endless is _____ an end.

clueless	A detective who is clueless is _____ a clue.
valueless	A vase that is valueless is _____ value.
spiritless	A horse that is spiritless is _____ spirit.

What does the suffix *ed* mean?

Notice the underlined words in the sentences below. How does the addition of the suffix **ed** change the meaning of each word?

I smile today. I smiled yesterday.

You plant the onions. I already planted the tomatoes.

I work fast. I worked faster when I was younger.

You and I can walk together. We walked together many times in the past.

We should not talk on the phone as long as we talked before.

I help my sister. I helped her every day last week.

They listen to the radio all the time. They listened to their favorite program this morning.

What does the suffix *ness* mean?

Do you know what a noun is? A noun is a word that names a person, place, or thing. The thing named by a noun can even be an idea or a way of being.

Do you know what an adjective is? An adjective is a word that describes a noun.

The words in the list below on the left are adjectives. What happens to them when the suffix **ness** is added?

kind	kindness
sweet	sweetness
good	goodness
quick	quickness
nice	niceness
fine	fineness
fair	fairness

Use each of the pairs of words in a sentence or two to show that you understand their meanings.

What does the suffix *ment* mean?

Do you know what a verb is? A verb is a word that shows action. As you know, a noun is a word that names a person, place, or thing.

The words in the list below on the left are verbs. What happens to them when the suffix **ment** is added?

enjoy	enjoyment
treat	treatment
announce	announcement

punish   punishment
assess   assessment
pay   payment
develop   development
harass   harassment
govern   government

Use each of the pairs of words in a sentence or two to show that you understand their meanings.

What does the suffix *ly* mean?

Add the suffix **ly** to the underlined adjective in each example. Fill in the blanks with the new words formed. Can you explain what the suffix **ly** means? Find some other adjectives and make up more examples to solve.

My niece sang in a sweet manner.
She sang _____.

The boys played together in a nice manner.
They played _____.

Glenn spoke in a rude manner.
He spoke _____.

The Hillestads celebrated in a happy manner.
They celebrated _____.

Mr. Potter read in a quiet manner.
He read _____.

The mother prayed in a hopeful manner.
She prayed _____.

Denise limped along in a painful manner.
She limped _____.

Ralph set the table in a beautiful manner.
He set the table _____.

The children served tea in a careful manner.
They served it _____.

Meg held the kitten in a gentle manner.
She held it _____.

The baby slept in a very peaceful manner.
He slept _____.

Daniel marched along in a brave manner.
He marched _____.

Manuel ran the race in a very quick manner.
He ran _____.

Pamela spoke in a very soft manner.
She spoke _____.

Willoughby Wizard's Wonder Words

Which one of the words in the list below does not make sense with the others?

canine

feline

bovine

porcupine

ursine

REFERENCE LIST OF SUFFIXES

The following is a list of some of the most commonly used suffixes. There are many, many others. As you and your child think of or discover additional suffixes, add them to the list.

Suffix	Meaning	Examples
able, ible, ble	can be done	likable, breakable
able, ible, ble	inclined to	peaceable, forcible
acy, cy	state of	infancy, democracy
ade	product	lemonade, marmalade
age	place of	orphanage, parsonage
age	process of	marriage, carriage
al	relating to	natural, familial
ance, ancy	state of	importance, vacancy
ant, ent	person who	migrant, student
ar	relating to	polar, muscular
ard, art	person who	drunkard, braggart
arian	person who	vegetarian, veterinarian
ation	action of	protestation, narration
ation	state of being	excitation, aggravation
cy, y	action of	piracy, perjury
dom	state of being	boredom, freedom
ectomy	surgical removal	appendectomy, tonsillectomy
ed	past tense	walked, shared
en	made of	wooden, golden
en	to make	darken, shorten

Suffix	Meaning	Examples
ence	condition of	dependence, confidence
er	more	higher, bigger
er, or	a person who	banker, sailor
ery, ry	place where	bakery, library
est	most	largest, greatest
et, ette	little	piglet, cigarette
eth	numerical order	thirtieth, fiftieth
fic	causing	horrific, odorific
ful	full of	beautiful, thankful
fy	make or cause	liquefy, unify
gram	writing or drawing	telegram, diagram
graph	written or drawn	photograph, phonograph
hood	condition, quality	childhood, sisterhood
ic	relating to	angelic, volcanic
ier, yer	person who	cashier, lawyer
ine	like	feminine, masculine
ing	present participle	doing, falling
ing	of a specific kind	bedding, siding
ion	act or process	construction, subtraction
itis	disease or inflammation	arthritis, tonsillitis
ive	having the nature of	negative, active
less	without	toothless, homeless
logy	the study of	biology, archeology
ly	like, in a specific way	kindly, foolishly
ment	thing or result	fragment, ornament
ment	action	government, punishment

Suffix	Meaning	Examples
most	superlative	topmost, outermost
ness	condition or state	tiredness, goodness
ory	place where	laboratory, conservatory
ous	having quality of	joyous, poisonous
some	like	quarrelsome, awesome
th	part of	fifth, tenth
ward	direction of	forward, westward
y	inclined to	rainy, sleepy

ADDITIONAL SUFFIXES

_____   _____   _____
_____   _____   _____
_____   _____   _____
_____   _____   _____
_____   _____   _____
_____   _____   _____
_____   _____   _____
_____   _____   _____

Willoughby Wizard's Wonder Words

Do you know what a plural is?
A plural is the form of a word
that means more than one.
Usually, a plural is formed by adding -s.
Dogs means "more than one dog."
Cats means "more than one cat."
But how do you say the plural form (more than one)
of the objects or animals on the list below?

deer	**mouse**
sheep	**goose**
leaf	**man**
knife	**woman**
elf	**child**
wife	**tooth**

Chapter 5

Synonyms, Antonyms, and Homonyms

SYNONYMS, ANTONYMS, AND HOMONYMS are important classes of words to consider when undertaking a study of vocabulary. They provide a means of categorizing words as they relate to one another. These relationships help make the words in each group easier to remember.

SYNONYMS

Synonyms (from the Greek *syn*—"like" + *onym*—"name") are words whose meanings are generally the same. By considering groups of words that are similar in meaning, your child will begin to be able to make distinctions between them and to use and understand words more precisely. For example, look at the list of synonyms below:

bad
awful
naughty
wicked

These words could certainly be viewed as synonyms. They all mean somewhat the same thing. However, there are some subtle differences in their meanings. Notice that sometimes the difference in meaning concerns degree or extent: I might have a *bad* headache, but an *awful* headache is even worse. Sometimes the difference might be in connotation: *Naughty* brings to mind a picture of a freckle-faced kid with his hand in the cookie jar, while *wicked* conjures up a much more sinister image.

Now consider these synonyms:

big
large
huge
gigantic
great

If you are very hungry, you might order a *big, large, huge,* or even a *gigantic* pizza. A *great* crowd might gather if the pizza were free, and a *great* white shark would probably like pizza of any size!

It is fun to compare synonyms and determine the fine distinctions between them. In the exercises that follow, encourage your child to choose a synonym from

Synonyms, Antonyms, and Homonyms

the list given to fill in each blank appropriately. Since the words are so similar in meaning, there may be more than one set of correct answers. Discuss your child's answers with her and ask her to explain and justify her choices.

dirty
filthy
grimy
messy

Johnny's room was _____.

Dad put the _____ pair of work pants into the washing machine.

The girls got _____ when they helped plant some seeds in the garden.

The old barn was full of _____ rats' nests.

happy
cheerful
jolly
glad
merry

I am _____ to tell you that today is my birthday.

Bonnie was _____ that the performance was over.

The circus clown was fat and _____ .

My grandmother always behaves in a _____ manner.

Mr. Johnson smiled at all his customers and wished them a _____ Christmas.

> cut
> snip
> chop
> trim

Angie asked the hairdresser to _____ her hair.

The recipe said to _____ the onions.

Mrs. Picciano used a small pair of scissors to _____ the loose thread on her blouse.

Clara will _____ out twenty-four valentines for her classmates.

Look at the synonym pairs below. In each pair, though the words have almost the same meaning, one has a generally positive connotation and the other has a generally negative connotation. Ask your child to decide which word is which. Again, discuss your child's answers and your reasoning.

proud	arrogant
ask	beg
pretend	imagine
bold	brazen
give	relent
cackle	giggle
sensitive	touchy

Synonyms, Antonyms, and Homonyms

Willoughby Wizard's Wonder Words

How many words can you find that are more interesting or descriptive synonyms for the word *said*? Here are a few to get you started.

whispered

yelled

murmured

answered

exclaimed

ANTONYMS

Antonyms (from the Greek *anti*—"against" + *onym*—"name") are words whose meanings are generally opposite. The study of antonyms provides an opportunity to compare and contrast concepts. Classifying words in this manner presents another way to think about how words relate to each other. Encourage your child to complete the following antonym exercises. Discuss the possible answers with your child.

Think of an antonym, or opposite, for each word listed below.

hot	fast
dry	clean
sweet	hard
bad	smart
sad	smooth
rich	tired
thin	wide
man	crooked
down	over
big	top
tall	little

Replace one word in each sentence below with an antonym that makes more sense.

The weak wind blew the big tree over.

The rude girl sent her grandmother a thank-you note.

The children enjoyed playing in the snow all summer.

The wealthy man had very little money.

After the rain, the streets were all dry.

The shy girl spoke loudly to the boy she had just met.

Craig wins many races because he is such a slow runner.

The wicked witch in the fairy tale always does something kind.

The puppy liked to lie on his hard pillow.

Choose the one word in each line that does not belong.

fast	slow	quick
dull	shiny	bright
chilly	cool	warm
soft	hard	downy
falsehood	fib	truth
thin	thick	wide
old	ancient	young
tiny	large	huge
fellow	guy	woman
lively	tired	sleepy
proud	meek	haughty
rough	smooth	slick
strong	powerful	feeble
elaborate	fancy	plain
loose	snug	tight
vacant	crowded	congested

HOMONYMS

Homonyms (from the Greek *homo*—"same" + *onym*—"name") are words whose names sound the same, but whose meanings are different. Exploring homonyms will help your child learn how to use these words appropriately and spell them correctly. Encourage your child to complete the following homonym exercises. Discuss your child's answers with him or her.

Match one homonym from each pair to the picture that illustrates its meaning.

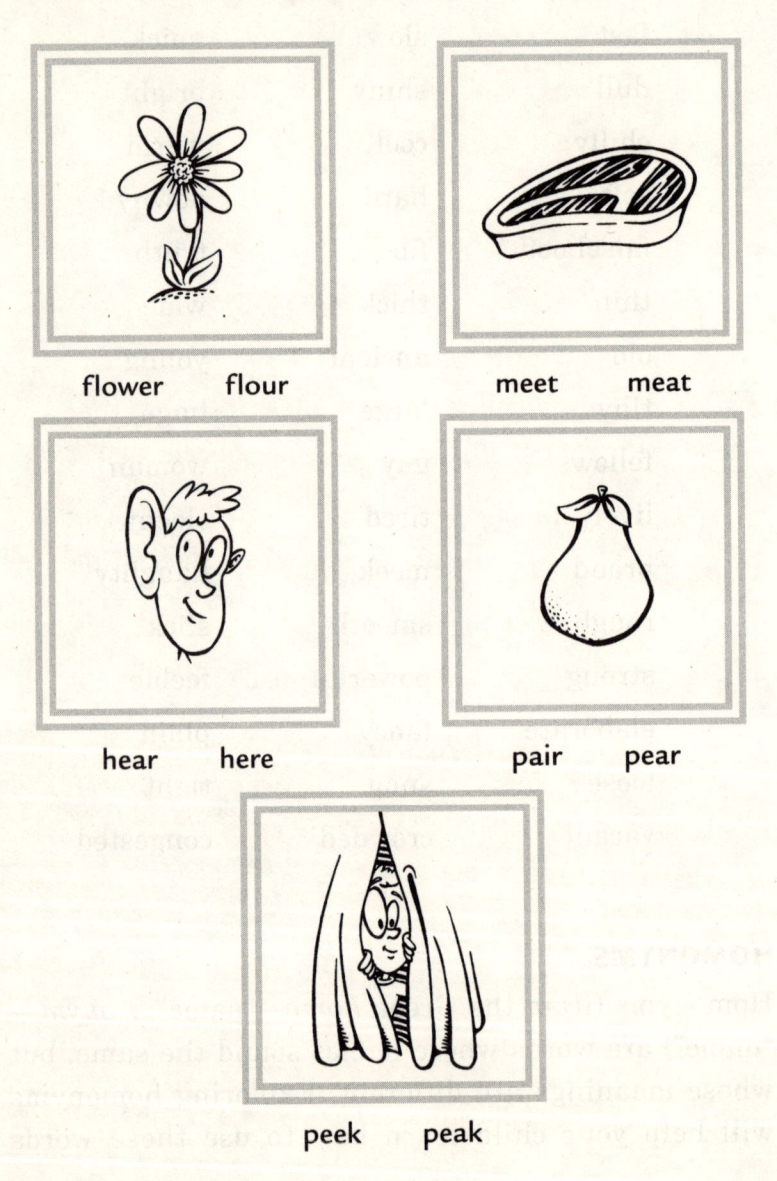

flower   flour   meet   meat

hear   here   pair   pear

peek   peak

Synonyms, Antonyms, and Homonyms

him   hymn   hair   hare

Think of a pair of homonyms that correctly completes each set of sentences.

The truck can _____ a lot of trash.
Our room is at the end of the _____.

The kitten was very _____ because it was so young.
I am going to spend a _____ on a ranch in Wyoming.

It is fun to _____ gifts in beautiful paper.
When it is time for dinner, my dad will _____ on the door.

The cut will _____ quickly if you keep it clean.
I got a blister on my _____ after that long hike.

81

I will put some decorations on the little _____ tree.

Many people consider it improper to wear _____ coats.

My _____ Jenny and Uncle Lou are coming to visit.

The little _____ carried a crumb that was larger than itself.

REFERENCE LIST OF HOMONYMS

Here is a generous sampling of some homonyms in the English language. As you and your child think of or discover additional homonyms, add them to the list.

aisle	isle	fair	fare
allowed	aloud	fir	fur
ant	aunt	flee	flea
ate	eight	flower	flour
bail	bale	gait	gate
bass	base	gilt	guilt
be	bee	grown	groan
beach	beech	guest	guessed
bear	bare	hail	hale
beat	beet	hair	hare
blue	blew	hall	haul
bore	boar	heal	heel
bow	bough	herd	heard
break	brake	here	hear
bury	berry	high	hi
by	buy	him	hymn
cash	cache	hole	whole
cell	sell	hour	our
cents	sense	in	inn
cheap	cheep	jam	jamb
chews	choose	knot	not
chute	shoot	know	no
close	clothes	knows	nose
creak	creek	leak	leek
dear	deer	led	lead
doe	dough	loan	lone
eye	I	loot	lute

made	maid	seem	seam
main	mane	sew	so
male	mail	shear	sheer
meet	meat	shone	shown
mince	mints	site	sight
moose	mousse	slay	sleigh
morn	mourn	soar	sore
new	knew	sole	soul
none	nun	some	sum
one	won	son	sun
pair pear	pare	stake	steak
pale	pail	stare	stair
pane	pain	steal	steel
pause	paws	sweet	suite
peak	peek	tale	tail
peel	peal	tea	tee
plain	plane	team	teem
poll	pole	tear	tier
pore	pour	their	there
pray	prey	threw	through
principal	principle	tide	tied
profit	prophet	time	thyme
quarts	quartz	to too	two
rain rein	reign	toe	tow
rap	wrap	vale	veil
red	read	vein vane	vain
reed	read	wait	weight
reel	real	waist	waste
ring	wring	we	wee
road	rode	weak	week
rose	rows	wood	would
sail	sale	write	right
see	sea		

Synonyms, Antonyms, and Homonyms

ADDITIONAL HOMONYMS

_____   _____
_____   _____
_____   _____
_____   _____
_____   _____
_____   _____
_____   _____
_____   _____
_____   _____

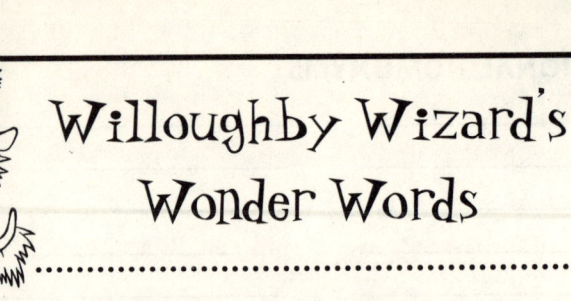

HOW TO DEVELOP YOUR CHILD'S GIFTS AND TALENTS IN VOCABULARY

Willoughby Wizard's Wonder Words

Sometimes words with very different meanings
have exactly the same spelling
and are pronounced exactly the same way.
Use the clues below and a dictionary
to help you find the following:

> **A word that means both
> a flower and a color.**
>
> **A word that means both
> a bird and a toy that flies.**
>
> **A word that means both
> a road and a fish.**

Can you find other examples
of words like these?

Chapter 6

Analogies

AN ANALOGY IS a very particular kind of comparison. It challenges the reader to discover a relationship between two words and then to apply this relationship to another set of words. It requires some high-level thinking skills as the reader must analyze each portion of the problem, using reason to determine just what relationship is exposed. Look at the example below:

Ice is to cold as fire is to _____.

In this simple analogy the reader must first make the connection between the first pair of words: that cold is the principal attribute of ice. Then the reader must look at the second part of the analogy and find the missing word that relates to fire in the same way that cold relates to ice. The obvious answer is hot.

The words in analogies can relate in almost infinite ways. The first pair of words might mean the same thing, or they might be opposites. The analogy might relate to the characteristics or attributes of the item named, or to the uses or actions of those items. In the following exercises encourage your child to define the relationship between the first pair of words, then to seek the answer that best completes the analogy. Be prepared for some creative thinking on the part of your child. He may make connections that are not immediately obvious to you, so ask him to explain his reasoning process. Often, there is more than one answer that makes sense. Look for multiple solutions to the problems, then discuss the possibilities and determine which answer is best.

The first set of analogies involves the comparison of synonyms or antonyms.

>Love is to hate as stop is to _____.

>Little is to small as big is to _____.

>Down is to up as near is to _____.

>Fast is to slow as give is to _____.

>Happy is to cheerful as wealthy is to _____.

>Thin is to narrow as thick is to _____.

>Early is to late as young is to _____.

>Over is to under as bottom is to _____.

Analogies

In another type of analogy the first pair of words is linked because one of the words describes a characteristic or component of the other. Find a word that will complete the second part of the analogy in the same way.

For example:

Sugar is to sweet as lemon is to sour.

or

Day is to week as month is to year.

Pumpkin is to orange as grass is to _____.

Beach is to sand as ocean is to _____.

Milk is to cheese as flour is to _____.

Ounce is to pound as minute is to _____.

Blue is to sky as yellow is to _____.

Fur is to soft as shell is to _____.

Sometimes analogies compare a general group with a specific member of that group.

For example:

Bird is to robin as dog is to poodle.

A robin is a specific kind of bird. A poodle is a specific kind of dog. Any particular breed of dog would correctly complete the analogy.

Consider each analogy carefully to determine whether the general or specific term comes first!

Broccoli is to vegetable as apple is to _____.

Basketball is to game as taffy is to _____.

Chevrolet is to car as Nike is to _____.

Tree is to oak as insect is to _____.

Furniture is to table as flower is to _____.

New York is to city as Kansas is to _____.

Hammer is to tool as plate is to _____.

Trumpet is to instrument as Appaloosa is to _____.

Animal is to cat as plant is to _____.

Feeling is to joy as color is to _____.

Vehicle is to car as shirt is to _____.

Crocodile is to reptile as cow is to _____.

Nation is to France as beverage is to _____.

Grandmother is to relative as dictionary is to _____.

Toy is to ball as fish is to _____.

Food is to hamburger as gem is to _____.

Analogies

Willoughby Wizard's Wonder Words

These are words that are used to describe a whole group, set, or type of objects. Can you think of some of the objects that might belong in each group?

instruments

sports

vehicles

tools

clothes

A slightly different type of analogy is that which compares a whole object or group with one or more of its parts.

For example:

Star is to constellation as page is to book.

Claw is to crab as branch is to _____.

Toe is to foot as finger is to _____.

Class is to student as alphabet is to _____.

Paw is to cat as hoof is to _____.

Singer is to choir as player is to _____.

Scale is to fish as feather is to _____.

Key is to piano as string is to _____.

Kernel is to corn as petal is to _____.

Yet another type of analogy compares objects to related actions or functions.

For example:

Ball is to throw as bike is to ride.

Read carefully to make sure whether the object or the action comes first in each pair of words!

Boat is to float as airplane is to _____.

Write is to pencil as cut is to _____.

Sweep is to broom as drive is to _____.

Bed is to sleep as stove is to _____.

Eye is to see as ear is to _____.

Read is to book as listen is to _____.

Shovel is to dig as brush is to _____.

Some analogies compare objects to the places where they are generally found, such as:

Analogies

Honey is to hive as money is to bank.

Others compare objects that are usually thought of as belonging together:

Salt is to pepper as peanut butter is to jelly.

Again, study the relationship between the first pair of words to help you determine the most suitable answer to each analogy.

Sock is to foot as glove is to _____.

Farm is to cow as zoo is to _____.

Forest is to tree as library is to _____.

Ice cream is to cone as tea is to _____.

Mother is to father as sister is to _____.

Grape is to vine as apple is to _____.

Worm is to dirt as fish is to _____.

The analogies in this section are not separated by type. This makes them more difficult, as the connection in each initial pair of words must be deciphered without any hints or clues. Look for all the types of analogies that have previously been covered and maybe some new ones, too!

Horse is to neigh as dog is to _____.

Hat is to head as shoe is to _____.

Short is to long as beginning is to _____.

Cat is to kitten as sheep is to _____.

Cake is to bake as house is to _____.

Pillow is to soft as rock is to _____.

Ice cream is to cold as soup is to _____.

Tree is to bark as orange is to _____.

Paper is to staple as board is to _____.

Cup is to drink as fork is to _____.

Fly is to bird as gallop is to _____.

Good is to bad as polite is to _____.

Warm is to hot as cool is to _____.

Clock is to time as thermometer is to _____.

Knife is to chef as stethoscope is to _____.

Plain is to fancy as easy is to _____.

Baby is to infant as taxi is to _____.

Safety is to danger as peace is to _____.

Analogies are frequently seen on vocabulary tests. They can be useful in determining the test-taker's understanding of the subtle differences between words. Start now to help your child become familiar and comfortable with word problems in this format and the thought processes used to solve them. Make up additional analogies for him to solve, or look in your library or bookstore for books that feature these puzzles.

Analogies

Willoughby Wizard's Wonder Words

Each word in the left-hand column is related in some manner to one or more of the words in the right-hand column. Find as many connections as you can.

white	desert
hot	popcorn
wet	towel
dry	snowflake

Chapter 7

Figures of Speech

A FIGURE OF SPEECH is a word or an expression that means something other than the literal interpretation of that word or expression. Usually, figures of speech invoke colorful or interesting images and serve to liven up both conversation and written passages. However, they can be confusing to the unwary reader. Some knowledge about the various types of figures of speech is valuable and will help your child better comprehend what she reads. Encourage your child to explore the examples that follow the discussion of each figure of speech.

PERSONIFICATION

Personification is the assigning of personal or human characteristics to objects or ideas. To describe the wind as angry or a flower as cheerful is to use personification. Neither wind nor flowers have feelings, but both these descriptions conjure up a particular response in the reader. To say that duty calls or love beckons is to use personification. Duty is a concept, an idea, as is love. Neither love nor duty has a voice with which to call or beckon, but these figures of speech give each concept more power.

Here are a few more examples of personification:

Mother Earth

whispering pines

fortune smiles

lady luck

blind justice

a laughing brook

HYPERBOLE

Hyperbole is the use of exaggeration for effect. The exaggeration is generally extreme, so that the statement could not possibly be the literal truth. For example, a rich woman might be said to have all the money in the world. Of course, this is immediately recognizable as hyperbole, as, indeed, no one person could have all the money in the world. However, this figure of speech readily conveys to the reader that the woman is far beyond "wealthy" or "rich."

Some other examples of hyperbole include:

> The baby is as fat as a pig.
>
> Gloria waited an eternity for the bus to come.
>
> Johnny was hungry enough to eat a horse.
>
> The little girl cried her heart out.
>
> I fell to pieces when I heard the news.
>
> We almost laughed our heads off.

METONYMY

Metonymy is the substitution of a related word for the name of the person or thing that is meant. For example, when we refer to the press, we don't mean a printing press, we mean the reporters and writers for newspapers and magazines. When we say that the country is in mourning, we mean that the people of the country are grieving, not the country itself. A bad apple is said to spoil the whole barrel when, indeed, it spoils the other apples and leaves the barrel unharmed. Each of these uses of metonymy add interest and emphasis to the ideas they express.

In each example of metonomy below, your child should determine what person or thing is represented by the underlined word or phrase.

> Joey was excited when he got his <u>wheels</u>.
>
> <u>The White House</u> issued a statement about the war.
>
> The man could not turn away from his own <u>flesh and blood</u>.

The <u>bleachers</u> erupted when the home team scored.

The <u>school office</u> issued a list of rules.

<u>The university</u> planned its orientation for the end of August.

The criminal could not evade <u>the law</u>.

SIMILE AND METAPHOR

Simile and metaphor are among the most commonly used figures of speech. Simile is the direct comparison between two things. Similes often include the words *like* or *as,* per the examples that follow:

She is as pretty as a picture.

He moves quietly, like a cat.

Metaphor draws a comparison by substituting one object for another, as in these examples:

Her heart was a bass drum, beating

wildly in her chest.

The night was a symphony of insect

noises.

In the following sentences your child should decide whether each contains either a simile or a metaphor.

The thunder rumbled like a runaway train.

Ellen was as meek as a lamb.

James became a tiger when he put on his football uniform.

The President is an actor on the stage of history.

A flood of phone calls poured in.

Grandpa said the new baby was as cute as a button.

EUPHEMISM

Euphemisms are expressions that are used to take the place of an unpleasant idea, as follows: A worker might be terminated instead of fired; a person is said to have passed away instead of died; a used car might be referred to as preowned. In each case the use of the euphemism seeks to cast a more positive light on a somewhat negative event or idea and make it more palatable.

The problem with euphemisms is that in time, the euphemism takes on the negative meaning and has to be replaced with yet another euphemism. For instance, once people with physical disabilities were called crippled. This word fell out of favor and was replaced with the word *handicapped.* Now *differently abled* is the preferred term. In time, this term may give way to yet another phrase.

In the euphemisms that follow help your child to restate the meaning of each underlined word or phrase in a more direct or blunt manner.

He <u>stretched the truth</u>.

The ladies were <u>perspiring</u> in the afternoon heat.

The fellow was <u>intoxicated</u>.

We had to have our dog <u>put to sleep</u>.

I went to the dentist to have a tooth <u>extracted</u>.

Mr. Lassiter was <u>detained by the police</u>.

That outfit is <u>not very flattering</u>.

LITOTE

A litote is an affirmative statement that is made by negating its opposite. For instance, someone who is commenting positively on the weather might say, "The weather is not at all unpleasant today." Or, one might compliment a friend by saying, "Your golf game certainly hasn't gotten worse since last week!"

Encourage your child to explain the meaning of these litotes:

The General Sherman is no small tree.

Amber was not a bit unhappy with her new furniture.

The smell of bread baking is far from unpleasant.

Pamela's engagement ring was not cheap.

The quarterback's role in Sunday's victory was not unimportant.

CLICHÉ

Sometimes a figure of speech is so colorful or appropriate that it comes into common usage. It is then referred to as a cliché. Our language is full of clichés, and these can present a real challenge to those for whom English is a second language, as well as for youngsters. Though these sayings may be familiar to adult ears to the point of tedium, they are likely to prove mysterious to a child who is meeting them for the first time. For example, if you say "Uncle Joe is in hot water," your child may picture him soaking in a Jacuzzi. If you state that Joe should "face the music", your little one might picture him looking toward an orchestra or the speakers of his stereo set.

Read each phrase below and the accompanying sentence to your child. Ask her to take a guess as to the meaning of each cliché. Discuss the difference between the literal interpretation and the common usage of the cliché.

turn the tables
My uncle likes to play practical jokes, so we decided to turn the tables and play a joke on him.

make a beeline
When it is lunchtime, the hungry children make a beeline to the cafeteria.

take the bull by the horns
Jeremy dreaded cleaning his room, but his sister advised him to take the bull by the horns and get it done.

born with a silver spoon in her mouth
Princess Maya was born with a silver spoon in her mouth.

let the cat out of the bag
The party was supposed to be a surprise, but Noella let the cat out of the bag.

put the cart before the horse
Heather wanted to go out and play before she did her homework, but her mother told her not to put the cart before the horse.

a fish out of water
When Danny went to the new school, he felt like a fish out of water.

on pins and needles
We were all on pins and needles as we waited to hear the results of the election.

read between the lines
Mary didn't tell us that she was unhappy, but we could read between the lines.

bite the bullet
Ron had to bite the bullet and tell his parents that he had misbehaved at school.

leave no stone unturned
Mrs. Ilves left no stone unturned in her search for her missing car keys.

burned his bridges
George burned his bridges when he quit his job without giving notice.

in the long run
Stacy was upset because she and Marisa had a fight, but Mother said that they would still be friends in the long run.

break the ice
The teacher played some funny games with his new students to help break the ice.

Keep a list of the clichés that you and your child encounter in reading and conversing. You will be amazed at how many there are and how often we rely on them to express ourselves. Although we try to avoid the use of clichés in most written communications, they are valuable in daily conversation.

Point out examples of simile, metaphor, hyperbole, and other figures of speech as you read with your child. Encourage him to create figures of speech of his own. Staple some blank sheets of paper together to form a booklet. On each page write a figure of speech and ask your child to draw a picture that illustrates its meaning.

Increasing your child's awareness of all sorts of figures of speech and their meanings will help to deepen her understanding and appreciation of language.

Chapter 8

Where Do Words Come From?

WE KNOW THAT our language developed from ancient sources and has its roots deep in the past, but we also realize that it continues to change and evolve. New words come into common usage and old words become obsolete and slip quietly away. Where do words come from and where do they go?

Let's look at the origins of some words we hear every day. For example, how did the days of the week get their names? Each name, of course, contains the word *day*. This word derives from an ancient word which meant "the time of the sunshine," referring to the period of light between sunrise and sunset. Sunday was named by the Romans in honor of the sun. Monday, similarly, was named for the moon. The Anglo-Saxons

HOW TO DEVELOP YOUR CHILD'S GIFTS AND TALENTS IN VOCABULARY

Willoughby Wizard's Wonder Words

There are words and phrases that have come directly from Latin and are still in use. Here are just a few of the most common ones and their meanings.

in loco parentis
  in the place of a parent

in memoriam
  in memory of

status quo
  the existing state of affairs

vice versa
  with the order changed

modus operandi
  manner of operation

terra firma
  dry land, solid ground

per diem
  by the day, for each day

retained the Roman names for Sunday and Monday, but Tuesday, Wednesday, and Thursday were named after the Anglo-Saxon (and Norse) gods Tiw, Woden, and Thunor respectively. Friday is named for Frigga, the wife of Woden, who was the goddess of marriage, and Saturday for Saturn, the Roman god of agriculture.

The names of the months of the year also derive from the Latin of the Romans. January was named for Janus, who was the Roman god of beginnings and endings. Janus could look back to the past and forward to the future because he had two faces. The new year is often a time of reflecting on the year gone by and planning for the year ahead, so Janus is a fitting symbol for this month!

February's name derives from the Latin *februare,* which means to "cleanse or purify." At one time, long ago, Romans considered February to be the last month of the year. They recognized March 1 as the beginning of the New Year, and February was their time to tidy up and prepare for a new start.

March, the beginning of spring, was the month when Romans prepared to go off to war, so they named the month in honor of Mars, the god of war.

April's name comes from the Latin word meaning "to open," since the earth seemed, in the Romans' northern climate, to burst open with life and growth at this time.

May was probably named for Maia, the Roman goddess of spring, and June for Juno, the goddess of marriage. June is still the most popular month in which to be married!

July is named in honor of Julius Caesar, a Roman emperor, and August for Augustus, his nephew, who succeeded him.

HOW TO DEVELOP YOUR CHILD'S GIFTS AND TALENTS IN VOCABULARY

Willoughby Wizard's Wonder Words

What's in a Name?

Some names have been in use for many, many years. They come from root words that had particular meanings. Is your name on this list?

Name	Root Language	Meaning
Adam	Hebrew	man of red earth
Alexander	Greek	helper and defender
Amy	French	beloved
Daniel	Hebrew	God is my judge
Deborah	Hebrew	the bee
Dennis	Greek	god of wine
Elizabeth	Hebrew	consecrated to God
Heather	Middle English	the heather flower
Jessica	Hebrew	wealthy one

Where Do Words Come From?

More Willoughby Wizard's Wonder Words

Name	Root Language	Meaning
John	Hebrew	God is gracious
Julia	Latin	youthful one
Laura	Latin	a crown of laurel leaves
Lynn	Old English	from the waterfall
Margaret	Latin	a pearl
Matthew	Hebrew	gift of Jehovah
Michael	Hebrew	who is like God
Nicole	Greek	victorious
Sarah	Hebrew	princess
Thomas	Greek	a twin
William	Old German	protector
Zoe	Greek	life

The remaining months are named for the position they held in the order of months during ancient Roman times. When March marked the beginning of the new year, September was the seventh month, October the eighth, November the ninth, and December the tenth. The Latin words for *seven, eight, nine,* and *ten* are *septem, octo, novem,* and *decem.*

Does your child like to eat cereal for breakfast? Cereal is named for the Roman goddess of agriculture, Ceres. The Romans often made offerings of grain to Ceres in gratitude for their successful crops. While the word *cereal* actually refers to the seeds produced by grasses such as wheat, oats, and corn, as you may know, we call the products made from them cereal, too.

You can explain to your child that the box that cereal comes in, the pages of this book, and lots of other things are made of paper. The word *paper* comes from Egypt. The Egyptians wanted something to write on that was not as heavy and unwieldy as clay tablets. They found a way to use a plant that grew along the Nile River. They sliced or mashed the plant and flattened it into thin sheets. When the sheets dried, they were thin, light, and strong. Our word *paper* comes from the name of that plant—*papyrus.*

One place where a lot of paper is used is at your child's school. The word *school* has a Greek root, *schole,* which means "leisure." Your child may think of school as a great deal like work, but the ancient Greeks liked to spend their leisure hours listening to a teacher and talking about the world. This was their form of education. Gradually, the word *schole* came to stand for a place where these discussions occurred. Now, of course,

Willoughby Wizard's Wonder Words

Some words and many place names in our language were given to us by the Native Americans. Here are a few. Can you find more examples?

> **squash**
>
> **moccasin**
>
> **Mississippi**
>
> **powwow**

the word *school* refers to any establishment for the purpose of learning.

When your child leaves to go to school each morning, he says good-bye to you and the rest of your family. *Good-bye* is actually a compressed form of the phrase "God be with ye." Over time, the longer phrase was replaced with our shorter version.

Not only do old words take on new forms, as seen in the case of good-bye, but sometimes brand-new words are needed. For example, when Alexander Graham Bell invented a device that enabled people to talk to each other from great distances, he needed a name for it. He used some Greek words: *tele,* which means "far," and *phone* which means "sound." He put them together to create a word that most of us know all too well—*telephone.* Other words formed in this way include *microscope, automobile,* and *television.* Many medical and technical words are created in this manner whenever they are needed to describe a new product or a procedure.

Another way that words come into being is through the use of acronyms. Acronyms are single words formed by using the initial letters or syllables of the words in a descriptive phrase. The military is fond of acronyms, and many that were created by the army and navy have found their way into common usage. For example, the word *jeep* came from *GP,* or "general-purpose vehicle." *Scuba* gets its name from the much lengthier "self-contained underwater breathing apparatus."

The *zip code* we use on every piece of mail stands for "Zoning Improvement Plan," while *laser* stands for "light amplification by stimulated emission of radiation." Acronyms have been readily accepted because they are so much easier to say and to remember than the lengthy phrases they replace.

Sometimes two words are blended together to form a new, more descriptive word. These are called portmanteau words. *Smoke* and *fog* are blended to give us *smog.* A meal that occurs in the midmorning is neither *breakfast* nor *lunch,* but *brunch.* And a cross between *motorist* and *hotel* yields *motel.*

Where Do Words Come From?

Willoughby Wizard's Wonder Words

Many of the words we use were derived from people's names. Here are just a few. Look them up to learn what they mean and why they were given these particular names.

cardigan

boysenberry

pasteurize

watt

zeppelin

sandwich

HOW TO DEVELOP YOUR CHILD'S GIFTS AND TALENTS IN VOCABULARY

Willoughby Wizard's Wonder Words

Sometimes two complete words are joined together to form a new word. These are called compound words. What is the meaning of each compound word below? Can you think of other words like these?

driftwood

slowpoke

overalls

butterfly

treehouse

flagpole

seashore

Over time, many words keep their same forms but change in meaning. For example, the familiar word *deer* used to refer to any creature with four legs. Now we know it as a particular animal. *Maid* used to mean "girl," but it is now more likely to refer to someone who performs domestic services. *Villain* used to mean "farmer," but now it refers to a much more sinister person. *Starve* once meant "to die from any cause," whereas now it means "to die or suffer from lack of food."

Another mechanism for the altering of the meanings of words or the creation of new words is slang. Slang words are usually colorful and unconventional, and they are often fresh or humorous.

Sometimes slang words are newly created terms, such as *moola* (money) or *nerd* (a person who fails to fit into the social scene). More often, though, slang expressions are familiar words to which an unconventional meaning is attached. For instance, to *rip off* in conventional speech means "to tear something away." In slang it means "to steal." Other examples of words and expressions with both conventional and slang usages include *hot, cool, dude, drip, turkey,* and *flake.*

Each generation develops its own slang words, some of which disappear after a short period of popularity and others which move into more standard usage. Here is a list of a few American slang terms from the last fifty years. Discuss the list with your child and determine which ones are still in use today.

groovy	sting	nitty-gritty
far-out	trip	rubberneck
radical	sap	scram
dough	man	skiddoo

bag   pad   ham
dig   threads   grub
klutz   dish   hunk

Because our language is forever growing and changing, there will always be new words to learn and new meanings to attach to old words. The process of acquiring vocabulary is an endless one, and it can be a source of enjoyment for people of all ages. In the next chapter you will be introduced to a variety of games that will keep you and your family involved in this lasting process of learning about, and loving, words.

Willoughby Wizard's Wonder Words

Contractions are shortened forms of words or phrases. An apostrophe is placed in the word to denote the location of the letter or letters that have been removed. Match each contraction on the left to its longer form on the right.

can't	he is
doesn't	are not
hadn't	is not
he's	let us
I'll	who is
isn't	she will
let's	you are
might've	can not
she'll	does not
they've	had not
you're	we are
who's	might have
we're	they have
aren't	I will

Chapter 9

Games to Play with Words

THIS MAY BE the single most useful chapter in the book. Here you will find a wide assortment of games you can play with your child. Some of them are commercially produced, others require a few simple materials, and some require nothing at all except a little bit of time. What they have in common is that they are all built on a foundation of words and they are fun. Because they are fun, they are effective! Try as many of the games on the list as possible. Find the ones that your family most enjoys and play them regularly. Your child will get the message that words are enticing, interesting, and entertaining. Keep a dictionary or two nearby—and enjoy!

COMMERCIAL GAMES

Scrabble®

Two or more players

This pioneer of word games has been around for a very long time but never grows old. There is a junior version that is fine for the younger set, but if you can only purchase one, make it the standard version. Instead of playing competitively, play cooperatively. Keep a running, combined score for all players and see how many points you can accumulate together in any one game. This is an important variation, as it allows each player to participate on every turn. All players examine each other's letters to help find the best word possible. Players at varying levels can participate without frustration.

It will also be valuable to purchase a Scrabble® dictionary, available in paperback form, for quick reference. Store it in the box with the game so that it will always be handy when you play.

Pictionary®

Two or more players

Pictionary® is a bit like charades on paper. One person from each team reads a secret word on a card and tries to draw it for his teammate to guess before the timer runs out. There is a junior edition of this game as well. Many of the words are familiar, but the act of converting the words into pictures requires players to think deeply about their meanings. It is helpful to have a neutral party available to whom a young player can go for explanation of a word that he or she does not understand.

Balderdash®

Four or more players

Balderdash® is ideal for older kids (about fourth grade and up) and adults. It is like the old parlor game of Dictionary. A word that no one in the group is likely to know is read by one person. Everyone else makes up a definition for the word, writes it down, and passes it to the reader. The reader then reads aloud all of the made-up definitions, as well as the correct definition. All players then guess which is the correct definition. This game provides lots of laughs and practice in writing, practice in creative thinking, and exposure to brand-new words. Most of the words in this game are obscure and will likely be forgotten soon after the game ends. Still, some of them will stick, and a great deal of vocabulary learning will take place in the process of playing the game and hearing the definitions, both real and fabricated.

Scattergories®

Two or more players

A large, many-sided die is rolled to reveal a letter of the alphabet and to start the game. Players must think of words beginning with that letter which fit into several categories, such as "things at the beach," "colors," and "farm animals." This requires players to think about the relationships between words, and, of course, the answers of other players will often introduce new ideas and vocabulary.

A timer is used to keep the game moving. This is more appropriate for older children who can write quickly.

Boggle®

Two or more players

This game is played with letter dice that are placed in a plastic grid in a random arrangement. Players then use a word-search technique to create lists of words before the sand runs out in the hourglass. Play can be made easier for little ones by allowing them credit for three-letter words, while older players can be limited to five- or six-letter words, or by giving younger players extra time. Again, these modifications allow for successful interaction of players with a variety of ability levels. In this way, the younger players learn a great deal. Take a little extra time as you go over your lists at the end of each round to show young players where to find each word in the grid and what it means.

This is a great way for kids to learn about suffixes and prefixes, as identifying these word parts within the grid helps to build their lists.

PENCIL AND PAPER GAMES

Jotto

Two or more players

Each player needs a sheet of paper and a pencil. All players should write the alphabet across the bottom of their piece of paper. The player who is "it" writes a five-letter word across the top of his paper, making sure that the other players cannot see it. Perhaps the word chosen is *house*.

Each player takes turns calling out a five-letter word. "It" compares the word given to his own word. For example, a player might give the word *bring*. Since this word has no letters in common with his word, "it" will say "zero." Now the players can mark off the letters *B-R-I-N* and *G* on their alphabet, for they know that the word "it" has chosen contains none of these letters.

Each player, including "it," should keep a list of words called and number of letter matches in each word. Players use the information gained with each word called to deduce the word "it" has chosen. When a player calls out the exact word, "it" must answer, "Jotto!"

Sample Jotto Sheet
(It selects this word) *house*

Players guess:	It answers:
bring	0
grins	1
tiger	1
right	1
plate	1
steal	2
horse	4
house	Jotto!

a b c d e f g h i j k l m n o p q r s t u v w x y z

(Players mark off letters on the alphabet as they are eliminated. Players then incorporate eliminated letters in their guess words in order to figure out the selected word.)

Password

Five players

You will need a pencil and some small slips of paper. One player is chosen as the word giver. The other four players form teams of two. The word giver writes the same word on two slips of paper and gives a slip to one member of each team. The team members with the words take turns giving their partners clues about the words. Each clue must consist of one word only and must relate to the word in some way.

Here is a sample of play. Let's say the word is *birthday*.

The first clue given is *party*.	(If the word is guessed correctly on the first clue, that team receives ten points.)
The next clue given is *cake*.	(If the word is guessed correctly on the second clue, that team receives nine points.)
The next clue might be *presents*.	(If the word is guessed correctly on the third clue, that team receives eight points, and so on. If the word is not guessed after ten clues, the word giver reveals the word and a new round is started.)

Play continues through a predetermined number of words or until a predetermined score is reached.

Vocabulary Speed

Two or more players

You will need pencils and paper for this game and a watch or a timer. Each player is given a piece of paper and a pencil. The timekeeper sets a time limit—say thirty seconds—and calls out a letter of the alphabet. The players then write down all the words they can think of that begin with the letter. Players should take turns being the timekeeper.

You can modify the game for a variety of ability levels by allowing younger players to use words of three and four letters and requiring older players to use words of greater length, perhaps five or even six letters.

Hangman

Two or more players

Paper and pencils, or chalk and a chalkboard are needed for this game. Almost everyone knows how to play Hangman, but it is a perennial favorite and so deserves mention. The player who is "it" selects a secret word and draws a line for each letter of the word on a piece of paper. He also draws a scaffold. He writes the alphabet across the bottom of the paper. The other players take turns guessing letters that may be in the word. If a player correctly guesses a letter, "it" writes the letter in the appropriate space. If a player guesses incorrectly, "it" draws one body part of a stick figure on the scaffold. The object is to correctly guess the word before a complete body is drawn.

Although this game is not effective at introducing entirely new vocabulary, it is a great way to reinforce words that have been introduced but which have not become completely familiar.

Word Hunt

Go for a walk or a drive with your child. Take along a pad of paper and a pencil. Write down all the words you find on signs. Look for words that begin with a certain letter or end with *-ing*. Look for rhyming words or words written in red. There are many different kinds of word hunts, and as you do a few you will come up with new ideas of your own.

When you get home, go over the list and circle all the words that your child does not know. Help your child to learn those words. Work together to make up a story that includes all the words on your list.

Hinky Pinky

Two or more players

This is a game of rhyming riddles. The person who is "it" thinks of two words that rhyme and make sense as a phrase, such as *fat cat*. "It" then gives the other players a two-word clue, using a synonym for each of the words in the rhyming pair. In this case the clue might be *chubby kitten*. "It" makes the game a little easier by announcing whether the rhyme is a hink pink (one syllable in each word), a hinky pinky (two syllables in each word), or a hinkety pinkety (three syllables in each word) before giving the clue. Rhymes can have up to three syllables or a mixture of syllable lengths.

More examples:
- *Clue:* This is a hink pink—large porker.
- *Rhyme:* big pig
- *Clue:* This is a hinky pinky—silly dollar.
- *Rhyme:* funny money
- *Clue:* This is a hinky pinkety—fake sandwich meat.
- *Rhyme:* phoney baloney

Going to Grandpa's House

Two or more players

The first player begins by saying, "I'm going to Grandpa's house and I am going to take _____." (The player must name an item; for example, a pencil.) The second player must say, "I'm going to Grandpa's house and I am going to take a pencil (naming the item mentioned by the first player) and a _____." Let's say this player says "a cupcake." The next player must say, "I'm going to Grandpa's house and I'm going to take a pencil, a cupcake, and a _____." Play continues in this manner until players are tired of the game or want to start a new one. If someone can't remember an item, give him or her a clue. Give the game an added twist by requiring that the first item begin with *A,* the next with *B,* etc.

While this game may or may not introduce new words depending on the contributions of other players, it does provide great practice at memorization, which is a generally helpful skill. It also focuses the attention of the players on words. Adult players should make a point of including words that may be unfamiliar to the younger players.

Categories

Two or more players

The game begins when one person names a category, let's say "flowers." The first player names a flower, such as "daisy." The next player must name another flower, such as "rose." Play continues until a player is stumped or repeats an item already mentioned. This game will encourage players to dig deeply into their store of words to retrieve some that may not be used every day.

Whatchamacallit

Odd tools or household gadgets, especially old ones, can be the source of an interesting game. Show one (or a picture of one) to your child and ask him to guess what the use of the object is or was. Encourage creativity and fantasy. The object here is to elicit lots of vocabulary, not to come up with a right answer. This is a fun party game, too, with participants voting for the "best" explanation. Garage sales and junk stores often yield some great Whatchamacallits.

Sometimes you may know the origin of the object and a serious discussion about its use can introduce lots of new words and ideas. For example, the examination of an old milk can might elicit words such as *dairy, churn, pasteurize, homogenize,* and so forth.

Picture Window

Cut out a number of pictures from magazines. Create the picture window by cutting a small (2" x 2") window out of a sheet of cardboard or construction paper. Lay this over the picture so that only the portion in the window is showing. Ask your child to guess what the picture shows based on the portion she can see through the window. Discuss what the picture might be, then look to see.

Choose pictures with subjects that you think will serve to generate some interesting new words.

Transformations

This is a very old word game, but it is still challenging and fun. The object is to transform one word into another by changing one letter at a time. The words often are opposites or are related, but the only firm rule is that they must be of the same length. Here are some examples:

> Turn **heat** to **cold.**
> (**heat** head held hold **cold**)

> Turn **pig** to **cow.**
> (**pig** pog pow **cow**)

Sometimes it takes only a few changes to achieve the transformation, but other times it takes many.

> Turn **rain** to **snow.**
> (**rain** gain grin grim gram cram craw crow brow blow slow **snow**)

Can you solve this one in fewer steps? Nonsense words are not allowed! Try making up some transformations of your own for your whole family to solve!

Dollar Words

Any number of players

Each player needs a paper and a pencil. Calculators and dictionaries for each player are helpful but not essential. Make sure each player can see the following chart:

A	1	N	14
B	2	O	15
C	3	P	16
D	4	Q	17
E	5	R	18
F	6	S	19
G	7	T	20
H	8	U	21
I	9	V	22
J	10	W	23
K	11	X	24
L	12	Y	25
M	13	Z	26

The object of the game is to find words whose letter values add up to exactly 100. This is a great ongoing challenge. Post a list of all the dollar words your family finds and add to it as more are discovered.

Make a Word

Any number of players

Each player needs a paper and a pencil. A timer might also be useful to keep the game moving along quickly. Each player takes a turn naming a rather long word. Allow use of the dictionary to ensure the selection of interesting words. Each player writes the word at the top of his or her paper. The timer is set to an agreed-upon time, and all players work to find and write down as many words as possible that can be formed using only the letters in the selected word. An example follows.

Rumpelstiltskin

rum	simple	ink
rumple	limp	lump
stilt	skimp	skull
skin	plum	smell
tilt	sputter	kin

When the time is up, compare lists to see who has found the most words. To level the playing field, allow younger children to give answers using two- or three-letter words, older children words of four or five letters or more, and limit adults to words of five or six letters or more!

Word Pyramids

Any number of players

Each player will need a pencil and a sheet of paper. Or use a chalkboard or a large sheet of paper to play the game cooperatively. Begin with any letter. Write it at the top of the page or board. This will be the top of your pyramid. Below this letter, write a two-letter word that contains that letter, like this:

O

T O

Next, find a three-letter word that contains both letters from the previous word:

T O P

Continue in this way until you can add no more levels to the pyramid.

P O E T
P O E T S
P O S T E R

Compare pyramids to see who was able to create the largest one.

Hint: Some letters are not desirable as starting letters! Why not?

Games to Play with Words

Willoughby Wizard's Wonder Words

Anagrams

Anagrams are formed when
the letters of a word are rearranged
to form a new word.
Rearrange the letters of each word below
to make a different word.

rate

lump

fowl

team

stop

grin

Willoughby Wizard's Wonder Words

Palindromes

Palindromes are words, phrases, or even whole sentences that read the same from right to left or from left to right. Here are a few examples. Can you find more?

Names
Hannah, Anna, Otto

Words
level, dad, radar, kayak

Phrases and Sentences
Mr. O. was a worm

A man, a plan, a canal—Panama

Word Grids

Two players

Each player needs a pencil and paper and must draw a 5" x 5" grid. Players then take turns calling out a letter and placing it anywhere on their grids. Letters may be called more than once.

Sample of play:

PLAYER ONE

	A	B		
S	T	E	M	

PLAYER TWO

			M	
	B	A	T	S
			E	

Player one: A
Player one: B
Player one: E

Player two: T
Player two: S
Player two: M

Play continues until each space on the grid is filled. Players try to form as many words as possible, both vertically and horizontally, as they enter the letters onto their grids. It is important to call both consonants and vowels. Finished grids might look like this:

137

HOW TO DEVELOP YOUR CHILD'S GIFTS AND TALENTS IN VOCABULARY

PLAYER ONE

L	A	B	R	Y
S	T	E	M	S
T	P	G	I	T
O	N	J	N	A
P	O	W	E	R

PLAYER TWO

N	R	G	M	L
I	P	R	O	A
J	B	A	T	S
N	O	P	E	T
Y	W	E	S	T

Scoring:

5-letter word—7 points

4-letter word—4 points

3-letter word—3 points

2-letter word—2 points (Allow only the youngest players to score points for 2 letter words.)

Only the longest word in each row or column of the grid is scored.

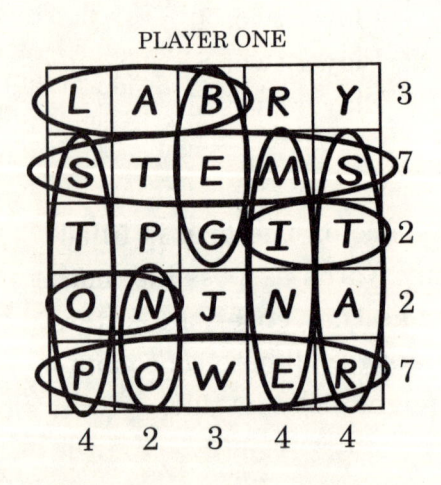

PLAYER ONE

(grid with circled words, row scores: 3, 7, 2, 2, 7; column scores: 4, 2, 3, 4, 4)

Total Score: 38

PLAYER TWO

(grid with circled words, row scores: 0, 3, 4, 4, 4; column scores: 0, 3, 7, 7, 4)

Total Score: 36

138

Games to Play with Words

Acronymble

One or more players

Choose any name, topic, or idea. Use the letters of the name as an acronym and then create a phrase or a sentence to describe the acronym. Players may disregard small connecting words such as *of, and, to,* and *the*.

> wolf—wild outlaw living free
> school—scads of children having obvious opportunities to learn
> pie—pleasure in eating
> swim—soak while increasing muscle

If more than one player is participating, take turns suggesting the name or topic and then compare results. There is no winner or loser, only lots of laughs and mental exercise.

Stretch a Word

Two or more players

One player is chosen to start the game. She gives a letter, say *A*. The next player must add a letter, making sure that it forms a word, such as *at*. Play continues with each player adding a letter that spells a real word. In the simplest version letters may only be added to either end of the word.

Sample play:

> a   at   pat   spat   spats

For more advanced players, letters may be added to the middle of the word and the order of the letters may be rearranged.

Sample play:

> a   at   rat   star   stair   traits

In any case, play comes to an end when no player can think of another word.

Ghost

Two players

In this game also players take turns adding letters to build a word. A letter can only be added at the end of the previously given letter, and the object is to avoid completing a word. However, each player must have a real word in mind when he or she adds a letter. If one player doubts that the other is thinking of an actual word, that player can challenge. Make sure a dictionary is available as a final authority!

Sample play:

> Player one: **p**
> Player two: **r**
> Player one: **i**
> Player two: **z**   (thinking of the word *prize*)
> Player one: **e**

Player one must give the final letter and therefore loses the round. Player one is awarded a letter *G* (the first letter in ghost). If the same player loses the next round, he or she will collect an *H*. Play continues until one player has accumulated all five letters from the word *GHOST*.

Willoughby Wizard's Wonder Words

Here's a game called Please Pass the Peas. Add as many *P*s as are needed to complete each word or phrase below. You will have to figure out how many *P*s are missing and where they belong!

Words	Phrases
eer	lumlum
aaya	aleie
male	oodleuy
hay	aerlate

You can play this game with any letter. Use a dictionary to find words that contain any letter you choose. Write the words on a piece of paper, leaving out the letter you have chosen. Challenge a friend or a family member to complete your list.

HOW TO DEVELOP YOUR CHILD'S GIFTS AND TALENTS IN VOCABULARY

Willoughby Wizard's Wonder Words

Most of the words that begin
with the letters *sn-*
relate to ideas or objects
that are unpleasant in some way.
Some people think this is because
of the facial expression that results
when we form this sound.
It looks like a sneer, doesn't it?
Use your dictionary to look for words
to expand this list,
and also to find a few exceptions!

sneer

snitch

snob

sneaky

snake

snivel

snide

Games to Play with Words

Plain and Fancy

Four or more players, divided into teams

Each team needs paper, a pencil, and a timer. The teams each make a list of ten simple words on a sheet of paper. These words can be adjectives such as *happy* or *pretty*, nouns such as *friend* or *rain,* and verbs such as *walk* or *sleep.* The timer is set to an agreed-upon time, and the players on each team work together to think of a "fancy" synonym for each "plain" word. For example:

happy—jubilant	rain—precipitation
pretty—beauteous	walk—perambulate
friend—companion	sleep—slumber

Vary the length of time allowed according to the ability level of the group. Allow use of a dictionary and a thesaurus if desired.

Connections

Two or more players

To begin, one player names a word, such as *good.* The next player must think of a word that makes a connection with the previous word. For example, here the player might say "night." Play continues until a player is stumped. A new word is given and play begins again.

Sample play:

good night time out side line
up set back seat belt way

Appendix

Words to Know

THE FOLLOWING LIST contains words that your child should probably be familiar with by the time he or she is ready to enter junior high school. The list does not contain the simple words that you would assume a young child would already know. It may not include all of the more complex words your child has already mastered. Obviously, it cannot be a complete list! What it does do is provide a reference point for you, a core group of words to introduce to your youngster over a period of years to make sure that he or she is progressing toward a useful, interesting, and well-rounded vocabulary. Do not expect your child to know and use all of these words by any given point in time. Your goal is to introduce any of the words that may be unfamiliar, so that your child has at least an initial exposure.

Together, go over only a few words from the list at any one sitting. Challenge your child to define the words he knows or to use them in sentences. Try to think of additional forms of the word. What prefixes and suffixes can be added? What related words can be found in the dictionary or thesaurus? If your child is unsure of the meaning, help her look it up. Make these unfamiliar words "words of the week" and see how often they pop up in your child's reading and conversations with your child.

Each word on the list is preceded by this symbol: ○
Shade the symbol as follows to keep track of your child's understanding of each word.

○	◐	●
unfamiliar	**familiar**	**mastered**

A

- ○ abandon
- ○ abbey
- ○ abbreviate
- ○ abduct
- ○ abolish
- ○ abrasive

- ○ abroad
- ○ abrupt
- ○ absolute
- ○ absorb
- ○ abstain
- ○ absurd
- ○ abundant
- ○ abuse
- ○ abyss
- ○ academic

- ○ accelerate
- ○ accent
- ○ access
- ○ accessory
- ○ accommodate
- ○ accompany
- ○ accomplice
- ○ accord
- ○ accordian
- ○ accumulate

Words to Know

- ○ accurate
- ○ acquaint
- ○ acquit
- ○ acute
- ○ adapt
- ○ adder
- ○ addict
- ○ adequate
- ○ adhere
- ○ adjacent
- ○ adjust
- ○ administer
- ○ admire
- ○ admit
- ○ admonish
- ○ ado
- ○ adobe
- ○ adopt
- ○ adore
- ○ adorn
- ○ advance
- ○ advantage
- ○ advent

- ○ aerosol
- ○ affection
- ○ affirm
- ○ afflict
- ○ affluent
- ○ affront
- ○ aftermath
- ○ agency
- ○ agenda
- ○ agent
- ○ aggravate
- ○ aggression
- ○ aghast
- ○ agitate
- ○ agony
- ○ agriculture
- ○ ailment
- ○ aisle
- ○ ajar
- ○ akin
- ○ alabaster
- ○ albatross
- ○ albino

- ○ alcove
- ○ alert
- ○ alibi
- ○ alien
- ○ align
- ○ allegiance
- ○ allergy
- ○ allied
- ○ altar
- ○ alter
- ○ alternate
- ○ altitude
- ○ amateur
- ○ ambassador
- ○ amber
- ○ ambition
- ○ amble
- ○ ambush
- ○ amend
- ○ amid
- ○ amiss
- ○ amphibian
- ○ ample

147

HOW TO DEVELOP YOUR CHILD'S GIFTS AND TALENTS IN VOCABULARY

- ○ amplify
- ○ amputate
- ○ amulet
- ○ amuse
- ○ anaconda
- ○ analyze
- ○ ancestor
- ○ ancient
- ○ anguish
- ○ animate
- ○ animosity
- ○ anniversary
- ○ annual
- ○ antagonize
- ○ antenna
- ○ anticipate
- ○ antifreeze
- ○ antique
- ○ antiseptic
- ○ antler
- ○ anxious
- ○ apology
- ○ apostrophe

- ○ appall
- ○ apparatus
- ○ apparel
- ○ appetite
- ○ applause
- ○ apply
- ○ appoint
- ○ appreciate
- ○ apprentice
- ○ approval
- ○ approximate
- ○ aquatic
- ○ arbor
- ○ archaic
- ○ archery
- ○ architecture
- ○ archive
- ○ arena
- ○ arid
- ○ aristocracy
- ○ ark
- ○ armor
- ○ array

- ○ arrive
- ○ arrogant
- ○ arsenic
- ○ arson
- ○ artery
- ○ article
- ○ artificial
- ○ artillery
- ○ ascend
- ○ aspire
- ○ assail
- ○ assassinate
- ○ assault
- ○ assemble
- ○ assert
- ○ asset
- ○ assist
- ○ associate
- ○ assortment
- ○ assume
- ○ assure
- ○ astonish
- ○ asylum

Words to Know

- atheist
- athlete
- atmosphere
- atone
- atrocious
- attain
- attempt
- attend
- attire
- attitude
- attorney
- attract
- auction
- audible
- audience
- auger
- authentic
- authority
- autumn
- avalanche
- average
- avid
- avoid

- awe
- awkward
- awning
- axle
- azure

B

- babble
- bachelor
- bacteria
- baffle
- balcony
- bale
- balk
- ballad
- ballet
- ballot
- balmy
- bandage
- banish

- banister
- bankrupt
- banner
- banquet
- baptize
- barb
- bargain
- barge
- barnacle
- barometer
- barracks
- barrage
- barren
- barricade
- barrier
- barter
- bashful
- basic
- basin
- baton
- batter
- bazaar
- beacon

- ○ beckon
- ○ bedlam
- ○ beggar
- ○ begrudge
- ○ belated
- ○ belfry
- ○ belittle
- ○ belligerent
- ○ bellow
- ○ benefit
- ○ benign
- ○ bereave
- ○ berth
- ○ betray
- ○ betroth
- ○ beware
- ○ bewilder
- ○ bicker
- ○ bind
- ○ biology
- ○ bizarre
- ○ blanch
- ○ blare

- ○ blemish
- ○ bliss
- ○ blithe
- ○ blizzard
- ○ blossom
- ○ blot
- ○ bluff
- ○ blunder
- ○ blunt
- ○ blur
- ○ blurt
- ○ boast
- ○ boisterous
- ○ bolt
- ○ bombard
- ○ bond
- ○ bondage
- ○ bonnet
- ○ bonus
- ○ boost
- ○ booth
- ○ botch
- ○ bough

- ○ boulder
- ○ bound
- ○ boundary
- ○ bounty
- ○ bouquet
- ○ bracket
- ○ braille
- ○ bramble
- ○ brass
- ○ brawny
- ○ brazen
- ○ breed
- ○ brew
- ○ bribe
- ○ brief
- ○ brilliant
- ○ brim
- ○ brink
- ○ brisk
- ○ bristle
- ○ brittle
- ○ broad
- ○ broil

Words to Know

- bronze
- brooch
- brood
- broth
- brow
- browse
- brutal
- budge
- budget
- bugle
- bulb
- bulge
- bulk
- bulletin
- bundle
- buoy
- bunting
- burden
- burnish
- burrow

C

- cache
- cadence
- café
- cajole
- calculate
- caliper
- callous
- camouflage
- campaign
- cancel
- candid
- canine
- canopy
- cantankerous
- capable
- capacity
- caper
- capsize
- caption

- captive
- carafe
- carcass
- caress
- carnivore
- cascade
- casual
- catastrophe
- cathedral
- caution
- cavalry
- cavern
- cavity
- cease
- celestial
- cement
- cemetery
- censor
- centennial
- ceramic
- certify
- chafe
- chaff

151

- ○ chalet
- ○ chamber
- ○ channel
- ○ chant
- ○ chapel
- ○ character
- ○ charity
- ○ chaste
- ○ chat
- ○ chef
- ○ chemical
- ○ cherish
- ○ chime
- ○ choir
- ○ chore
- ○ chowder
- ○ churn
- ○ chute
- ○ cinder
- ○ citizen
- ○ clamor
- ○ clarify
- ○ classify
- ○ clatter
- ○ clerk
- ○ clever
- ○ climate
- ○ cluster
- ○ coddle
- ○ coil
- ○ coincidence
- ○ colander
- ○ collaborate
- ○ collapse
- ○ collision
- ○ colony
- ○ column
- ○ combat
- ○ combustion
- ○ comical
- ○ commence
- ○ comment
- ○ communicate
- ○ comparison
- ○ compartment
- ○ compete
- ○ complex
- ○ compliment
- ○ compose
- ○ conceal
- ○ conclude
- ○ concrete
- ○ condemn
- ○ condense
- ○ conduct
- ○ confess
- ○ confide
- ○ confine
- ○ conform
- ○ confront
- ○ congested
- ○ congregation
- ○ conquer
- ○ conscience
- ○ consent
- ○ consequence
- ○ conserve
- ○ consider
- ○ console

Words to Know

- construct
- consume
- continue
- contrary
- controversial
- convince
- cord
- cordial
- corral
- council
- counsel
- courage
- courtesy
- cozy
- crafty
- crater
- crave
- crescent
- crevice
- cringe
- crucial
- crude
- cultivate

- culture
- cunning
- curious
- current
- custom
- cyclone
- cylinder

D

- dabble
- dainty
- dam
- dangle
- dank
- daring
- dawdle
- dawn
- daze
- dazzle
- deaf

- debate
- debt
- decay
- decent
- declare
- decline
- decorate
- dedication
- deed
- defeat
- defend
- defy
- degree
- delay
- deliberate
- delicate
- deliver
- demand
- demolish
- dense
- deny
- depart
- depend

- ◯ depress
- ◯ depth
- ◯ descend
- ◯ desert
- ◯ desire
- ◯ despair
- ◯ desperate
- ◯ destiny
- ◯ destroy
- ◯ detach
- ◯ detail
- ◯ detain
- ◯ detect
- ◯ determine
- ◯ detour
- ◯ develop
- ◯ devote
- ◯ devour
- ◯ diagonal
- ◯ dictator
- ◯ diet
- ◯ dignity
- ◯ dilemma

- ◯ disaster
- ◯ discipline
- ◯ disgust
- ◯ disk
- ◯ dispute
- ◯ distinct
- ◯ distress
- ◯ disturb
- ◯ divine
- ◯ docile
- ◯ dominant
- ◯ donate
- ◯ doom
- ◯ dormitory
- ◯ doubt
- ◯ dowel
- ◯ draft
- ◯ drama
- ◯ drastic
- ◯ dreary
- ◯ drench
- ◯ drift
- ◯ drizzle

- ◯ drone
- ◯ drought
- ◯ drowsy
- ◯ dual
- ◯ duct
- ◯ dull
- ◯ dusk
- ◯ duty
- ◯ dwelling
- ◯ dwindle

E

- ◯ eager
- ◯ earnest
- ◯ easel
- ◯ echo
- ◯ eclipse
- ◯ ecology
- ◯ economy
- ◯ ecstasy

Words to Know

- edit
- education
- efficient
- eject
- elastic
- elder
- elect
- electricity
- elegant
- elevate
- eliminate
- elude
- embark
- embellish
- embrace
- emerge
- employ
- emulate
- enchant
- encounter
- endurance
- engulf
- enhance

- enormous
- enthusiastic
- entire
- envy
- equipment
- eradicate
- erode
- errand
- erupt
- escapade
- escort
- essence
- establish
- estimate
- eternity
- ethics
- ethnic
- evade
- evaporate
- event
- evolve
- exact
- examine

- exceed
- excellent
- excess
- exchange
- exclaim
- excuse
- exhale
- exhaustion
- exhibit
- exist
- expand
- expense
- expert
- expire
- express
- exquisite
- external
- extreme

F

- ○ fable
- ○ fabric
- ○ failure
- ○ faint
- ○ faith
- ○ fake
- ○ false
- ○ familiar
- ○ famine
- ○ fanatic
- ○ fang
- ○ fantasy
- ○ fashion
- ○ fasten
- ○ fatigue
- ○ faulty
- ○ favor
- ○ feasible
- ○ feast
- ○ feature
- ○ federal
- ○ feeble
- ○ felony
- ○ fender
- ○ ferry
- ○ festival
- ○ fetch
- ○ feud
- ○ fiasco
- ○ fiction
- ○ fidget
- ○ fierce
- ○ figure
- ○ filament
- ○ filter
- ○ final
- ○ flinch
- ○ fixture
- ○ fizzle
- ○ flammable
- ○ flavor
- ○ flee
- ○ fleece
- ○ flesh
- ○ flexible
- ○ flimsy
- ○ floppy
- ○ florist
- ○ flourish
- ○ fluent
- ○ fluid
- ○ flurry
- ○ fluster
- ○ focus
- ○ foible
- ○ foliage
- ○ forfeit
- ○ forge
- ○ forlorn
- ○ formal
- ○ formula
- ○ fortunate
- ○ fossil
- ○ foul
- ○ foundation

Words to Know

- fraction
- fracture
- fragile
- fragment
- fragrance
- frantic
- fraud
- frenzy
- frequent
- friction
- frolic
- frothy
- frugal
- frustration
- fuel
- fumble
- function
- fund
- fundamental
- funeral
- funnel
- furnace
- furrow

- fury
- futile

G

- gab
- gadget
- gait
- gale
- gallery
- gallon
- garland
- garment
- gasp
- gaudy
- gauge
- gavel
- gawk
- gaze
- gelatin
- general

- generous
- gentle
- genuine
- germ
- gesture
- geyser
- ghetto
- glacier
- glamorous
- glance
- glare
- glaze
- gleam
- glimmer
- glimpse
- glisten
- gloat
- gloom
- glory
- glossy
- glutton
- gnarled
- gobble

HOW TO DEVELOP YOUR CHILD'S GIFTS AND TALENTS IN VOCABULARY

- ◯ gondola
- ◯ goof
- ◯ gorgeous
- ◯ gossip
- ◯ gouge
- ◯ govern
- ◯ gown
- ◯ graceful
- ◯ grammar
- ◯ grant
- ◯ grasp
- ◯ gratitude
- ◯ gravity
- ◯ graze
- ◯ greed
- ◯ grieve
- ◯ grill
- ◯ grime
- ◯ grind
- ◯ grip
- ◯ groan
- ◯ groom
- ◯ grudge

- ◯ grumble
- ◯ guarantee
- ◯ guardian
- ◯ guilt
- ◯ gulf
- ◯ gulp
- ◯ gust
- ◯ gutter

H

- ◯ habit
- ◯ habitat
- ◯ hack
- ◯ haggard
- ◯ hail
- ◯ halo
- ◯ halt
- ◯ hamper
- ◯ hangar
- ◯ harass

- ◯ harbor
- ◯ harsh
- ◯ harvest
- ◯ hasty
- ◯ hatch
- ◯ haughty
- ◯ haul
- ◯ haunt
- ◯ havoc
- ◯ hazard
- ◯ haze
- ◯ heap
- ◯ hearty
- ◯ heave
- ◯ hedge
- ◯ hefty
- ◯ heirloom
- ◯ helm
- ◯ hem
- ◯ herb
- ◯ heredity
- ◯ hermit
- ◯ hesitate

Words to Know

- hibernate
- hideous
- highlight
- hilarious
- hinder
- hinge
- hire
- history
- hitch
- hoard
- hoarse
- hoax
- hoist
- hollow
- honest
- honor
- hoof
- horizontal
- horrible
- horror
- host
- hostile
- humane

- humble
- humid
- humor
- hurdle
- hurl
- hurricane
- hustle
- hydrant
- hymn
- hypnotism

I

- ideal
- identify
- ignite
- ignorant
- illustration
- image
- imagination
- imitation

- immediate
- immigration
- impact
- import
- impostor
- impress
- improvement
- include
- increase
- individual
- industry
- infant
- inferior
- inform
- inherit
- initial
- injury
- innocent
- inspect
- instant
- instruct
- instrument
- insult

- ○ insulate
- ○ intelligent
- ○ intend
- ○ intense
- ○ interior
- ○ interview
- ○ introduce
- ○ invention
- ○ invitation
- ○ irritate
- ○ island
- ○ item

- ○ jealous
- ○ jeer
- ○ jest
- ○ jester
- ○ jetty
- ○ jewel
- ○ jiffy
- ○ jiggle
- ○ jitters
- ○ joint
- ○ joist
- ○ jolly
- ○ jolt
- ○ journal
- ○ journey
- ○ joyous
- ○ jubilant
- ○ judicious
- ○ jug
- ○ juggle
- ○ jumble
- ○ junction
- ○ junior

- ○ jury
- ○ justice
- ○ jut
- ○ juvenile

J

- ○ jab
- ○ jackpot
- ○ jagged
- ○ jalopy
- ○ jangle
- ○ janitor

K

- ○ kayak
- ○ keen
- ○ keg
- ○ kelp
- ○ kennel
- ○ kiln
- ○ kilt
- ○ kin
- ○ kindle
- ○ kink
- ○ knack
- ○ knell
- ○ knickknack
- ○ knit

Words to Know

- ◯ knob
- ◯ knoll
- ◯ knot
- ◯ knuckle

L

- ◯ label
- ◯ labor
- ◯ lack
- ◯ ladle
- ◯ lag
- ◯ lair
- ◯ lame
- ◯ lament
- ◯ lance
- ◯ landing
- ◯ landlord
- ◯ landscape
- ◯ landslide
- ◯ lank

- ◯ lantern
- ◯ lapse
- ◯ larder
- ◯ lather
- ◯ launch
- ◯ laundry
- ◯ lava
- ◯ lavender
- ◯ lawn
- ◯ lax
- ◯ leach
- ◯ league
- ◯ leak
- ◯ leap
- ◯ leash
- ◯ least
- ◯ leather
- ◯ lecture
- ◯ ledge
- ◯ leech
- ◯ leer
- ◯ legal
- ◯ legend

- ◯ leisure
- ◯ lend
- ◯ lengthy
- ◯ lenient
- ◯ level
- ◯ lever
- ◯ liberty
- ◯ license
- ◯ limb
- ◯ limit
- ◯ linger
- ◯ link
- ◯ lint
- ◯ liquid
- ◯ liter
- ◯ literal
- ◯ literature
- ◯ litter
- ◯ livestock
- ◯ loam
- ◯ loathe
- ◯ lobe
- ◯ local

M

- location
- locomotive
- lodge
- loft
- lofty
- loiter
- loot
- lope
- lore
- lounge
- loyalty
- lubricate
- luggage
- lumber
- lunge
- lurch
- luscious
- lush
- luxury

- madam
- magnificent
- magnify
- maiden
- maim
- maintain
- majestic
- major
- makeshift
- malice
- mallet
- mammal
- manage
- mangle
- maniac
- manicure
- mansion
- mantel
- mantle

- manufacture
- manure
- manuscript
- margin
- marriage
- marsh
- marvel
- masculine
- massage
- massive
- master
- material
- matter
- mature
- maze
- meadow
- meager
- mechanic
- medal
- medical
- mediocre
- meditate
- meek

Words to Know

- melancholy
- melody
- membrane
- memorial
- memory
- menace
- mend
- mental
- merchant
- mercy
- merge
- merit
- merry
- message
- metal
- meteor
- meter
- metric
- military
- mince
- mineral
- mingle
- miniature

- minimum
- minister
- minnow
- minor
- miracle
- mirage
- mirth
- mischief
- miser
- miserable
- mission
- mist
- mobile
- moccasin
- model
- moderate
- modern
- modest
- moist
- mold
- moment
- mongrel
- monk

- monument
- mood
- mope
- moral
- morsel
- mosaic
- motion
- motivate
- motive
- motor
- mound
- mourn
- mow
- muddle
- muffler
- mulch
- multiply
- multitude
- mumble
- mummy
- munch
- murky
- murmur

HOW TO DEVELOP YOUR CHILD'S GIFTS AND TALENTS IN VOCABULARY

- ○ museum
- ○ mushy
- ○ mute
- ○ mutter
- ○ muzzle
- ○ mystery
- ○ myth

N

- ○ nag
- ○ nape
- ○ narrate
- ○ narrow
- ○ nasty
- ○ national
- ○ native
- ○ natural
- ○ nature
- ○ nausea
- ○ navigate
- ○ navy
- ○ necessary
- ○ nectar
- ○ negative
- ○ neglect
- ○ negotiate
- ○ nephew
- ○ nervous
- ○ neutral
- ○ nibble
- ○ niche
- ○ niece
- ○ nimble
- ○ noble
- ○ nocturnal
- ○ nomad
- ○ nominate
- ○ nonfiction
- ○ nonprofit
- ○ nonsense
- ○ nook
- ○ noon
- ○ normal
- ○ notable
- ○ notice
- ○ notify
- ○ notion
- ○ notorious
- ○ nourish
- ○ novel
- ○ novelty
- ○ novice
- ○ noxious
- ○ nozzle
- ○ nudge
- ○ nuggat
- ○ nuisance
- ○ numerous
- ○ nursery
- ○ nurture
- ○ nutrition
- ○ nuzzle

O

Words to Know

- ○ oaf
- ○ oasis
- ○ oath
- ○ obedience
- ○ obese
- ○ object
- ○ obligation
- ○ oblong
- ○ obnoxious
- ○ obscene
- ○ obscure
- ○ observe
- ○ obstacle
- ○ obstruct
- ○ obtain
- ○ obvious
- ○ occasional
- ○ occupy
- ○ occur

- ○ odor
- ○ offend
- ○ offer
- ○ official
- ○ ogle
- ○ ogre
- ○ ointment
- ○ omelet
- ○ omen
- ○ omission
- ○ ooze
- ○ opaque
- ○ opera
- ○ operate
- ○ opinion
- ○ opponent
- ○ opportunity
- ○ opposite
- ○ optimism
- ○ option
- ○ orbit
- ○ orchard
- ○ orchestra

- ○ ordeal
- ○ ordinary
- ○ organism
- ○ organization
- ○ original
- ○ ornament
- ○ ornate
- ○ orphan
- ○ ought
- ○ outing
- ○ outlet
- ○ outline
- ○ overflow
- ○ overhaul
- ○ overly
- ○ overwhelm
- ○ oxygen

P

- paragraph
- parallel
- parasite
- parasol
- pace
- parcel
- pacific
- parch
- packet
- pardon
- padlock
- pare
- pageant
- parlor
- palace
- partial
- palette
- participate
- pallor
- particle
- palm
- partner
- pamper
- passenger
- pamphlet
- passion
- pandemonium
- pastel
- panel
- pastry
- panic
- pasture
- panorama
- patent
- pantomime
- patient
- pantry
- patriotic
- parade
- patrol
- paradise
- pattern
- pause
- peace
- peak
- peal
- pebble
- pedal
- peddle
- peer
- pellet
- penalty
- pendant
- penetrate
- pennant
- percent
- perfect
- performance
- perhaps
- perilous
- perish
- perk
- permanent
- permission
- perplex

Words to Know

- ○ persist
- ○ personal
- ○ personality
- ○ perspective
- ○ perspiration
- ○ persuade
- ○ pessimist
- ○ pest
- ○ pester
- ○ petty
- ○ phantom
- ○ phase
- ○ physical
- ○ pier
- ○ pigment
- ○ pillar
- ○ pilot
- ○ pinnacle
- ○ pioneer
- ○ pirate
- ○ pitiful
- ○ pity
- ○ pivot

- ○ plague
- ○ plaque
- ○ plaster
- ○ plaza
- ○ pledge
- ○ plenty
- ○ pluck
- ○ plume
- ○ plummet
- ○ plump
- ○ plunder
- ○ plunge
- ○ plush
- ○ poet
- ○ poker
- ○ policy
- ○ polish
- ○ polite
- ○ political
- ○ pollution
- ○ pompous
- ○ ponder
- ○ popular

- ○ population
- ○ port
- ○ portable
- ○ portion
- ○ portrait
- ○ position
- ○ positive
- ○ possess
- ○ possible
- ○ posture
- ○ potion
- ○ practical
- ○ prairie
- ○ prance
- ○ prank
- ○ precious
- ○ precise
- ○ predator
- ○ predicament
- ○ predict
- ○ prefer
- ○ prejudice
- ○ premium

HOW TO DEVELOP YOUR CHILD'S GIFTS AND TALENTS IN VOCABULARY

- ○ prepare
- ○ presence
- ○ preserve
- ○ pressure
- ○ prestige
- ○ presto
- ○ pretend
- ○ prevent
- ○ previous
- ○ prey
- ○ prickly
- ○ primary
- ○ primitive
- ○ priority
- ○ prism
- ○ prison
- ○ private
- ○ probably
- ○ probe
- ○ process
- ○ prod
- ○ product
- ○ profile

- ○ profit
- ○ progress
- ○ prohibit
- ○ promise
- ○ prompt
- ○ proper
- ○ proposal
- ○ prosper
- ○ protection
- ○ provide
- ○ provoke
- ○ prowl
- ○ public
- ○ publish
- ○ pucker
- ○ pudgy
- ○ puffy
- ○ pulp
- ○ pulse
- ○ puncture
- ○ pungent
- ○ punishment
- ○ puny

- ○ pupil
- ○ purchase
- ○ purpose
- ○ putter

Q

- ○ quaint
- ○ quality
- ○ quarrel
- ○ quarry
- ○ quart
- ○ quench
- ○ query
- ○ quibble
- ○ quill
- ○ quilt
- ○ quiver
- ○ quiz
- ○ quote

Words to Know

R

- ○ rabid
- ○ racket
- ○ radiant
- ○ radical
- ○ raffle
- ○ rage
- ○ rally
- ○ ramble
- ○ ramp
- ○ random
- ○ rapid
- ○ rapture
- ○ rascal
- ○ ration
- ○ ravine
- ○ react
- ○ reality
- ○ reap
- ○ reasonable

- ○ rebel
- ○ receipt
- ○ receive
- ○ recent
- ○ recipe
- ○ recite
- ○ reckless
- ○ reef
- ○ reel
- ○ reference
- ○ reflection
- ○ refreshment
- ○ regret
- ○ regular
- ○ rehearse
- ○ rejoice
- ○ relationship
- ○ relative
- ○ release
- ○ reliable
- ○ relief
- ○ reluctant
- ○ remedy

- ○ remnant
- ○ renew
- ○ repair
- ○ repeat
- ○ replica
- ○ represent
- ○ request
- ○ requirement
- ○ resemble
- ○ resent
- ○ reservation
- ○ residence
- ○ resign
- ○ resist
- ○ resource
- ○ respect
- ○ responsible
- ○ retain
- ○ retire
- ○ retreat
- ○ reveal
- ○ revenge
- ○ reverse

HOW TO DEVELOP YOUR CHILD'S GIFTS AND TALENTS IN VOCABULARY

- ○ review
- ○ revise
- ○ revive
- ○ revolution
- ○ reward
- ○ rhythm
- ○ ridge
- ○ rigid
- ○ rind
- ○ riot
- ○ risk
- ○ rival
- ○ robust
- ○ rodeo
- ○ romance
- ○ romp
- ○ roost
- ○ roster
- ○ rotate
- ○ rough
- ○ route
- ○ royal
- ○ rubble

- ○ rugged
- ○ rumble
- ○ rummage
- ○ rumor
- ○ rupture
- ○ rustle
- ○ ruthless

S

- ○ saber
- ○ sacred
- ○ sacrifice
- ○ salary
- ○ sallow
- ○ salute
- ○ sample
- ○ sandal
- ○ sane
- ○ sanitary
- ○ sarcastic

- ○ satisfactory
- ○ savage
- ○ scald
- ○ scamper
- ○ scan
- ○ scanty
- ○ scarce
- ○ scarlet
- ○ scatter
- ○ scene
- ○ scenery
- ○ scent
- ○ schedule
- ○ scheme
- ○ scholar
- ○ scold
- ○ scoot
- ○ scope
- ○ scorch
- ○ scorn
- ○ scour
- ○ scowl
- ○ scramble

Words to Know

- ○ scrap
- ○ scrape
- ○ scrawl
- ○ scrawny
- ○ screech
- ○ scribble
- ○ scroll
- ○ scuffle
- ○ sculpture
- ○ sear
- ○ secretive
- ○ section
- ○ security
- ○ seek
- ○ seize
- ○ select
- ○ sensible
- ○ sensitive
- ○ separate
- ○ sequence
- ○ serene
- ○ serious
- ○ service

- ○ settle
- ○ severe
- ○ shack
- ○ shallow
- ○ shame
- ○ shatter
- ○ sheaf
- ○ shear
- ○ sheer
- ○ shelter
- ○ shift
- ○ shimmer
- ○ shingle
- ○ shiver
- ○ shriek
- ○ shrill
- ○ shrink
- ○ shrivel
- ○ shrub
- ○ shudder
- ○ shuffle
- ○ shuttle
- ○ sigh

- ○ signal
- ○ significant
- ○ simmer
- ○ sincere
- ○ singe
- ○ singular
- ○ sinister
- ○ situation
- ○ sizzle
- ○ skein
- ○ sketch
- ○ skim
- ○ skimp
- ○ slack
- ○ slang
- ○ slant
- ○ slaughter
- ○ sleek
- ○ slick
- ○ slight
- ○ slim
- ○ slime
- ○ slink

- ○ slogan
- ○ sloppy
- ○ slouch
- ○ slumber
- ○ smother
- ○ smudge
- ○ snare
- ○ snatch
- ○ sneer
- ○ snort
- ○ snub
- ○ snug
- ○ snuggle
- ○ sober
- ○ society
- ○ socket
- ○ soggy
- ○ solemn
- ○ solid
- ○ solve
- ○ somber
- ○ soothe
- ○ sorrow

- ○ soul
- ○ spade
- ○ spar
- ○ spark
- ○ sparkle
- ○ sparse
- ○ spat
- ○ spatter
- ○ specific
- ○ speck
- ○ sphere
- ○ spigot
- ○ spike
- ○ spirit
- ○ spite
- ○ splendid
- ○ splint
- ○ sponsor
- ○ spouse
- ○ sprawl
- ○ spree
- ○ sprig
- ○ sprinkle

- ○ sprout
- ○ spunk
- ○ squad
- ○ squander
- ○ squat
- ○ squint
- ○ squirm
- ○ squirt
- ○ stagger
- ○ stain
- ○ stake
- ○ stale
- ○ stalk
- ○ stampede
- ○ stark
- ○ startle
- ○ starvation
- ○ statement
- ○ station
- ○ stationary
- ○ stationery
- ○ status
- ○ steady

Words to Know

- ○ stealthy
- ○ steep
- ○ steer
- ○ stem
- ○ stencil
- ○ stereo
- ○ sterilize
- ○ stitch
- ○ stoop
- ○ straddle
- ○ strain
- ○ strand
- ○ strategy
- ○ stray
- ○ streak
- ○ stress
- ○ stretch
- ○ stride
- ○ strike
- ○ stroke
- ○ struggle
- ○ stubborn
- ○ stumble

- ○ stunning
- ○ stunt
- ○ sturdy
- ○ stutter
- ○ subject
- ○ submerge
- ○ substantial
- ○ substitute
- ○ succeed
- ○ suction
- ○ suffering
- ○ suffocation
- ○ suggest
- ○ suitable
- ○ suite
- ○ sulk
- ○ summon
- ○ superb
- ○ supple
- ○ support
- ○ supreme
- ○ surface
- ○ surgery

- ○ surly
- ○ surrender
- ○ survey
- ○ survive
- ○ suspect
- ○ suspend
- ○ suspicion
- ○ swab
- ○ swagger
- ○ swamp
- ○ swarm
- ○ sway
- ○ swear
- ○ swell
- ○ swelter
- ○ swipe
- ○ swirl
- ○ swivel
- ○ swoop
- ○ symbol
- ○ sympathy
- ○ symphony
- ○ system

HOW TO DEVELOP YOUR CHILD'S GIFTS AND TALENTS IN VOCABULARY

T

- ○ tablet
- ○ tactic
- ○ tailor
- ○ talent
- ○ tamper
- ○ taper
- ○ tarnish
- ○ temper
- ○ temple
- ○ tempo
- ○ temptation
- ○ tenant
- ○ tender
- ○ tense
- ○ tentacle
- ○ terminate
- ○ terrain
- ○ terror
- ○ testify

- ○ tether
- ○ textile
- ○ thatch
- ○ theater
- ○ theme
- ○ theory
- ○ therapy
- ○ thimble
- ○ threat
- ○ thrive
- ○ throb
- ○ throne
- ○ thrust
- ○ tidy
- ○ tilt
- ○ title
- ○ token
- ○ tolerate
- ○ tonic
- ○ tornado
- ○ torrent
- ○ torture
- ○ total

- ○ tough
- ○ tourist
- ○ towering
- ○ trade
- ○ tradition
- ○ tragedy
- ○ trait
- ○ traitor
- ○ tranquil
- ○ transfer
- ○ transform
- ○ transparent
- ○ travel
- ○ tread
- ○ treasure
- ○ treaty
- ○ trek
- ○ tremble
- ○ trespass
- ○ tribe
- ○ tribute
- ○ trifle
- ○ trim

174

Words to Know

- triumph
- troop
- tropical
- trunk
- trust
- tube
- tuck
- tumble
- tunnel
- tusk
- tutor
- twinge
- twitch
- typical
- tyrant

- unique
- unison
- upholstery
- upright
- urban
- urge
- usher
- utensil
- utter

V

- vacant
- vaccine
- vacuum
- vague
- vain
- valid
- value
- vandal
- vanish

- vapor
- variety
- vault
- veer
- vehicle
- veil
- venom
- vent
- verse
- vertical
- veterinarian
- veto
- vibrate
- victim
- victory
- vigor
- villain
- violent
- visible
- vital
- vivid
- vocal
- void

U

- ultimate
- umpire
- union

HOW TO DEVELOP YOUR CHILD'S GIFTS AND TALENTS IN VOCABULARY

- ○ volume
- ○ volunteer
- ○ voyage

W

- ○ wade
- ○ wafer
- ○ wallet
- ○ waltz
- ○ wander
- ○ warehouse
- ○ warrior
- ○ waste
- ○ waterproof
- ○ weary
- ○ wedge
- ○ weird
- ○ wharf
- ○ wheeze
- ○ whimper
- ○ whine
- ○ whirl
- ○ whisker
- ○ whittle
- ○ whopper
- ○ wilderness
- ○ wisdom
- ○ witness
- ○ wizard
- ○ wobble
- ○ worship
- ○ worth
- ○ wrath
- ○ wreck
- ○ wrestle

X

- ○ xylophone
- ○ x-ray

Y

- ○ yacht
- ○ yam
- ○ yawn
- ○ yearn
- ○ yield
- ○ yodel
- ○ yolk
- ○ youth

Z

- ○ zany
- ○ zeal
- ○ zenith
- ○ zest
- ○ zone

Other books that will help develop your child's Gifts and Talents:

How to Develop Your Child's Gifts and Talents through the Elementary Years—Grades 1-5
$11.95/6 x 9/144 pp/paper/ISBN 1-56565-165-0

How to Develop Your Child's Gifts and Talents in Math
$15.00/6 x 9/176 pp/paper/ISBN 1-56565-338-6

How to Develop Your Child's Gifts and Talents in Reading
$15.00/6 x 9/224 pp/paper/ISBN 1-56565-447-1

101 Amusing Ways to Develop Your Child's Thinking Skills & Creativity
$13.00/6 x 9/208 pp/paper/ISBN 1-56565-479-X

Teach Your Child Math
$15.00/6 x 9/208 pp/paper/ISBN 1-56565-481-1

Teach Your Child Science
$12.95/6 x 9/192 pp/paper/ISBN 1-56565-347-5

Teach Your Child to Draw
$15.00/7 ½ x 9 ¼ /160 pp/paper/ISBN 0-929923-25-1

Thinking Games to Play with Your Child
$9.95/6 x 9/120 pp/paper/ISBN 0-929923-49-9

Available at your local bookstore. Or send a check or money order, plus shipping charges to:

Department PL
Lowell House
2020 Avenue of the Stars, Suite 300
Los Angeles, CA 90067

For special or bulk sales, call (310) 552-7555, ext. 30